The Quick Guide to
Therapeutic Parenting

also in the Therapeutic Parenting Books series

The Complete Guide to Therapeutic Parenting
A Guide to the Theory and What It Means for Day to Day Life
Sarah Naish and Jane Mitchell
ISBN 978 1 78775 376 1
eISBN 978 1 78775 377 8

Therapeutic Parenting Essentials
Moving from Trauma to Trust
Sarah Naish, Sarah Dillon and Jane Mitchell
ISBN 978 1 78775 031 9
eISBN 978 1 78775 032 6

The A-Z of Therapeutic Parenting
Strategies and Solutions
Sarah Naish
ISBN 978 1 78592 376 0
eISBN 978 1 78450 732 9

The Quick Guide to Therapeutic Parenting

A Visual Introduction

SARAH NAISH
AND
SARAH DILLON

Jessica Kingsley Publishers
London and Philadelphia

First published in Great Britain in 2020 by Jessica Kingsley Publishers
An Hachette Company

6

A CIP catalogue record for this title is available from the
British Library and the Library of Congress

ISBN 978 1 78775 357 0
eISBN 978 1 78775 358 7

Printed and bound in Great Britain by Clays Ltd, Elcograf S.p.A.

Jessica Kingsley Publishers' policy is to use papers that are natural,
renewable and recyclable products and made from wood grown in
sustainable forests. The logging and manufacturing processes are expected
to conform to the environmental regulations of the country of origin.

Jessica Kingsley Publishers
73 Collier Street
London N1 9BE, UK

www.jkp.com

Contents

Part 3: Ignorance Is Not Bliss: The Unhelpful Others

Part 4: Parenting in the Trauma Tornado

Part 5: SAFER Parenting: Therapeutic Responding

Part 6: Where Did *That* Come From?!

Acknowledgements

Thank you so much to Glynis, Liza, Jess, Angie, Emma, Rosie, Sair and Jane who helped to keep us laughing and inspired with their stories and flashes of inspiration! Also, and especially, thanks to Ray, who had to listen to hours of thinking out loud. You are all Therapeutic Parents Extraordinaire!

Introduction

SARAH NAISH

What is Therapeutic Parenting?

I like to use this definition of the term 'Therapeutic Parenting', which I have developed over the years.

> Therapeutic Parenting is a highly structured yet deeply nurturing parenting style, with a foundation of self-awareness and a central core of mentalization, developed from clearly held boundaries, with consistent, empathic, insightful responses to a child's distress and behaviours; allowing the child to begin to self-regulate, develop an understanding of their own behaviours and ultimately form secure attachments.

About this book

This book is intended to give parents, carers and supporting professionals an easy to follow, clear understanding of Therapeutic Parenting principles, often in a light-hearted way.

The use of analogies, pictures, catch phrases and memorable quotes throughout is central to the book's purpose; they are designed to provide you with an easy way to understand some of the most important concepts for Therapeutic Parents, and in a form that is quick and easy to reference.

It's intended to complement my other books. *The A–Z of Therapeutic Parenting* was written to be a one-stop reference providing solutions to common pitfalls and challenges faced by Therapeutic Parents. *Therapeutic Parenting Essentials: Moving from Trauma to Trust* was written to guide the reader through the *experience* of parenting therapeutically, including the perspectives of both parents and children, and drawing on my own life and experiences. *The Complete Guide to Therapeutic Parenting* (lead author Jane Mitchell) is for readers who want to dig deeper into the theory and research that lies behind Therapeutic Parenting.

The Quick Guide to Therapeutic Parenting is intended to be just that – an introduction for those new to Therapeutic Parenting, as well as a useful (and hopefully entertaining) source of inspiration for more experienced parents and carers.

It's the book which you can pass to your child's teacher or social worker, or to extended family to help them to grasp what Therapeutic Parenting is, how it works and just why it's so important!

Spreading the word about Therapeutic Parenting

Together, Sarah Dillon and I regularly run training and offer consultancy to individuals and organizations who are keen to learn about Therapeutic Parenting. Over the last few years, we have used analogies a great deal when trying to help worn-out parents to remember some key facts when caring for children with developmental trauma. This approach has been very successful and well received within our training.

In 2019, I established the Centre of Excellence in Child Trauma.[1] This effectively brought together all of our resources in training and support with the aim of helping to connect all Therapeutic Parents everywhere. This includes members of the National Association of Therapeutic Parents[2] from all over the world.

We now find that our members and readers are not just adopters and foster parents. We also have a wide number of birth parents, Special Guardians, step parents, and Kinship Carers too. The reason for this is that there is an increasing awareness that

---

1   www.coect.co.uk
2   www.naotp.com

Therapeutic Parenting is not just effective for children who come from abusive or neglectful starts in life. It is also effective for children who may have other difficulties, such as high anxiety, or issues arising from disability or prenatal stress.

Whatever your reason for picking up this book, we hope that it gives you some true lightbulb moments, some laughs and a feeling that you are not alone.

1

Why Do Our Children Do the Things They Do?!

When we speak at conferences, this is what we are asked about the most! Why does my child do the things he does? Why does she never seem to learn?

The key to changing our children's behaviours, and thereby making life a bit easier for everyone, is to understand the 'why'.

It's never straightforward, but if we remember that fear often masquerades as defiant anger we are off to a good start!

1

The Unskilled Pilot

(A Lack of Trust)

> Why is it so difficult for our children to trust me? After all I have shown them I can be reliable and won't hurt them.

So, the children were born on a plane. The plane took off (scary); they often couldn't see who was the pilot. The pilot was rubbish. Lots of turbulence, swooping, falling, lurching. The children didn't have a seat belt on and fell about all over the place. They got hurt. Sometimes the pilot couldn't be bothered to fly the plane. There were some quite dreadful crashes.

Then the airline moved them to *your* plane.

Brilliant! You are a good pilot. You regularly check on your passengers and know they are safely buckled in. You are sitting up front. You can see all the controls. You can see where you are going.

But the child can't.

All they know, all they remember, is the falling, crashing, and fear. They keep trying to break into the cockpit to fly the plane themselves, even though they don't know how to!

You are going to have to fly a long way, make loads of good landings and give tons of reassurance to your little passengers.

Then slowly, very slowly they will start to really let you fly their plane.

You are a Therapeutic Parent Pilot!

Until you prove yourself to be a capable pilot, your child won't trust you to fly their plane.

2

The Spider Parent

(Fear of Adults)

Why does my child follow me about but then push me away?

Think about something you are scared of.

It might be spiders, snakes, heights, rats or something else entirely.

How does it feel when you think about that fear? What physical and emotional symptoms do you experience?

Now think what you might do if that fear was inescapable. Perhaps you are trapped in a room with the spider. The spider is between you and the door.

What might you do?

Well, you may watch it very closely to see where it goes. You might try and trap it. Maybe you might even try and kill it if you can get close enough to it.

How might you feel?

Your heart might be banging. You might be sweating, breathing fast, or frantically looking for an escape route. You won't be thinking rationally.

How helpful might it be if someone comes along, sees you are scared and offers reassurance?

'Don't worry. It can't hurt you. It's only a spider!'

Does that make you feel better?

No! The fear is irrational. It's based in your lower brain and is instinctive.

You already *know* logically that the spider can't physically hurt you, but in **this** moment, in *this* fear it is irrelevant.

So, what if you were scared of adults?

The social worker (who is also a spider social worker and therefore cannot be trusted) has told the child that they are safe because she is taking them to live with lovely spider parents. These are good spider parents. Not like the last ones who hurt the child or scared them.

But they're still spiders.

What might the child do to feel safe?

They might follow the spider parents about. They might trap them. They might watch them carefully. They might try to control their movements or avoid them if they can.

Sound familiar?

If you are scared of spiders, you don't care if it's a good spider: Traumatized children are scared of adults!

3

My Friend the Spider

(Staying Safe)

> My child seems to have all the same interests as me and wants to spend time with me, but I feel like it's all fake. Why?

Your child might have been living with you since birth, or for just a short time. Thinking about the spider analogy in Chapter 2, you now know that you are *not only* the source of essential care for your child, but, where there has been trauma (caused by an adult), you may *also* be the source of fear.

Your child is dependent on their source of fear for their very survival.

They do not want the parent spider to hurt them or perhaps even kill them.

Maybe they were not abused in the strictest sense of the word, but perhaps they experienced medical interventions which they did not understand. Perhaps adults stuck needles in them while smiling reassuringly. The child did not know this spider doctor was being kind.

So, now they want to make sure you are not going to do the same. The best way to make sure you are not going to hurt them is to 'become' you. They want to 'be your friend'. If the abuser was a male abuser, then they are likely to work hard at befriending the biggest, most powerful male spider.

And yet... Instinctively you sense all is not well. That smile does not reach their eyes. When you try to get close, they pull away. There is a gap. Your gut tells you this is not genuine, and you are *right*!

Your child is letting the spider know that they are 'just like the spider' so it makes it harder for them to be hurt or forgotten about. Such a 'friendship' is driven by survival, not connection.

A parent may seek or expect parent/child 'intimacy' but the child is likely to resist this frightening 'into-me-see'.

4

The Automatic Car

(Illogical Behaviours)

My child does the most annoying things! I've tried asking him why he does it, but he won't answer!

Imagine you have been given a new car. This is very exciting, especially as it is an automatic car. You have never driven one before and you are looking forward to going for a drive.

All is going well until you have to turn left. You forget your car has no clutch and accidentally slam the brake hard, mistaking it for the clutch. Luckily all is ok, you just have a fright. Later that day you make the same mistake again and feel annoyed with yourself.

Then, your friend asks for a lift. They want to see your new car. You set off happily and are chatting away but you go to turn andoh no! The same thing happens again. Your friend nearly hits the windscreen!

'What are you doing?' your friend asks crossly.

You explain that the car is automatic and you've accidentally mistaken the brake for the clutch. You confess that you've done it a few times and keep forgetting. You apologize. You feel bad because you did not mean to scare your friend. You are annoyed with yourself.

Your friend tells you to just be careful and to jolly well make sure you remember next time.

Is that going to guarantee you never make this mistake again? No. Because the muscle memory of driving a car with gears for all those years is hardwired in.

Next time your friend is in the car, the same thing happens. Even though you were trying really hard and concentrating. You can't believe it. You haven't made this mistake for a month.

'Why did you do that!?' your friend shouts.

How do you feel? What might you say?

Asking our children 'why' lets them know that *we* don't have the answers and catapults them into shame about an instinctive behaviour they cannot control.

For example, a child left alone for long periods of time might chew their clothing or bedding to self-soothe.

You can either ask your child why they did something, or you can go in the kitchen and hit yourself over the head with a saucepan.

Both strategies are equally as effective.

5

The Plane Crash (Part 1)

(Impulsiveness)

My child is so naughty! She can be really aggressive and school say she won't sit still or even try to concentrate. We have tried talking to her, but nothing makes any difference.

Imagine you are on a plane. It is a long-haul flight and you are at the stage where it is all a bit dull. You are doing a crossword puzzle.

Suddenly, a voice from the cockpit says, 'Apologies but we are going to have to make an emergency landing due to a small fire in the back of the plane.'

Do you:

A. Sigh a little and continue doing your crossword puzzle?
B. Feel slightly anxious and tighten your seatbelt, abandoning the crossword puzzle?
C. Forget everything for now, feel panic-stricken and put all your energy into trying to survive?

My guess is C.

On a scale of 1–10 how important is it now that you finish the crossword puzzle?

The plane makes the emergency landing and you stand up to get off the plane quickly as you can see the fire at the back of the plane getting bigger. Unfortunately, a little old lady is standing in the way trying to get all her luggage out of the overhead locker. You swiftly move her out of the way and rush to the emergency slide.

Once you are off the burning plane, you stand at a safe distance feeling overwhelmed, shaky and hugely relieved. The cabin steward walks up to you and says crossly, 'Just now when we were evacuating the plane, you pushed that lady out of the way. I need you to sign an agreement to say that if ever this situation arises again you will not behave in such a way.'

You are dumbfounded. You don't reply as you feel the cabin steward might be confused and in shock.

Then he gets out a piece of paper and says, 'By the way, you dropped this crossword puzzle. I thought you might like to finish it.'

It is ridiculous, isn't it? No one would behave this way!
And yet they do. We do. Every single day.

Swap plane for school.
Swap crossword puzzle for school work.
Swap 'plane fire' to 'a person the child doesn't know suddenly entering the room.' (The adrenaline and cortisol spikes in the same way!)
Swap 'little old lady' for classmate.
Swap 'cabin steward' for teacher.

We expect our children to feel calm when they cannot calm, to concentrate and to behave rationally when they are in a fear state. Fight, flight, freeze, defensive rage. We then expect them to remember exactly what they did when in that state and to rectify it. It is ridiculous behaviour from *adults*!

It's not me, it's what *happened* to me. It's not *you*, it's what I've been through.

6

The Deal Breaker

(Breaking Promises)

> My child keeps running away or hurting people. Even when she knows it's wrong and has promised not to do it again!

Thinking about 'The Plane Crash' in Chapter 5, when you are pushing the little old lady out of the way, your higher brain (prefrontal cortex) is offline. All the energy is coming from your survival instincts. You are not learning, reflecting, using empathy or storing memories.

So, when the cabin steward then tries to make you agree not to behave in that way in the future, how can you do that? You will probably not even remember pushing the lady out of the way.

You may be looking at the cabin steward and thinking, 'Who is this freak? I need to just smile and nod to get him to leave me alone.'

Sometimes we waste *a lot* of time trying to 'reason' with a child when they *cannot* hear or process what we are saying.

Even though we can sign a contract saying we will not push the little old lady, (if ever we are exiting a burning plane again)... we *absolutely will!* Our thinking brain will be offline. Our survival brain, the amygdala, is in charge.

In the same way, if you are trying to elicit a promise or 'behaviour contract' agreement from a child because of an incident that happened when they were dysregulated, and their amygdala was in charge, be assured that they will smile and nod, agree with you and humour you. They will do whatever they need to do to survive that moment and make you go away. Then they can relax and go back to what they want to do.

During an incident, when the top (thinking) brain is offline, there is no point talking to the lower brain. It literally does not go in. When a child is dysregulated, their whole attention is on surviving the current crisis. They are not reflecting and thinking about the impact their behaviour has on you or anyone else for that matter...including themselves!

You can't do a deal with the amygdala!

7

The Land of Now

(Unable to Link Cause and Effect)

I've told him 100 times that if he steals from me, I will find out and there will be consequences. But he doesn't seem to care and just carries on!

The Land of Now is a wonderful place. The time on the clock always remains the same even though clearly things around me are changing. In the Land of Now I can do whatever I want. I can take the car keys and hide them to stop going to school right now.

I might eat lots of food. And then I might eat lots more because I can, because it's still now. Breakfast time is now, lunchtime is now, teatime is now, drink time is now, snack time is now.

In the Land of Now there are no consequences to anything I do! It's lovely!

Everything I need, I need now. There's no point me having it for tomorrow because I never see tomorrow. I only ever see now.

I can take this money because I need it now, and then I can see my friends and spend it now and make them happy now. I can't imagine what might happen to me about that because nothing exists – apart from now.

When we need to survive, we are only focused on our immediate needs. If we live in the Land of Now, it means that we will repeat the same mistakes over and over again and take a long time to learn. If our children live in the Land of Now, they don't care what happens to them in one hour, or one year.

The further away a consequence or reaction is from the event, the more meaningless it becomes:

A detention on Friday for rudeness five days ago. Pointless.
Taking away pocket money on Saturday for spoiling the sofa
    on Tuesday. Waste of everyone's energy.
A court appearance in July for an offence in February. Hopeless.

No synapses are being built. No connections being made. No bridges are being built between the Land of Now and the Land of Later.

We only know a child is beginning to heal when we see that they have empathy for their future self.

The beginnings of empathy are seen in the awakening of cause and effect thinking.

We know our children are making excursions from the Land of Now when their action *now* is moderated by what *might happen later*.

8

The Crumbling Wall

(Hidden Disabilities)

> My child looks like any other child but in reality she is *so* different. Surely this can't *all* be about a difficult start in life?

Imagine you have to build a wall for your child to thrive and grow. This is a very special wall. It is the wall of secure attachment. The foundation for life!

We will start with the bottom rows. What does a child need early on? Really essential stuff which they cannot survive without:

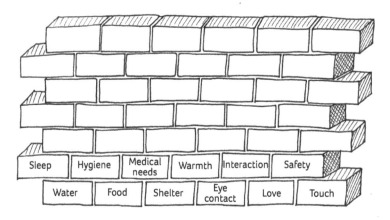

Sleep	Hygiene	Medical needs	Warmth	Interaction	Safety
Water	Food	Shelter	Eye contact	Love	Touch

With all these basic needs met, a child can relax and learn to trust adults to meet their needs. As they become more aware of their world and start to grow, we add more to the wall:

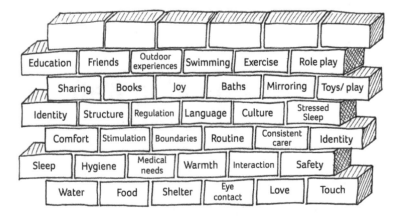

There are many other experiences our children have which form the building blocks of their development.

But what about a child who has suffered trauma?

It is tempting to think that some of the foundations might be a bit shaky and might need a make-over. Surely if we can put in 'Love' with enough 'Structure', our children should fairly quickly learn to trust and start healing?

We have overlooked an important aspect of this wall. Not only are the foundations shaky *but* some of the bricks aren't just missing, they have been replaced with others!

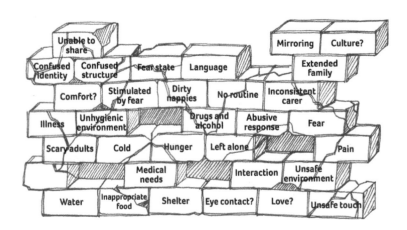

These building blocks are still building blocks. They are there, in the wall right in the middle of everything else. If we pull the bad bricks out, the whole wall might fall down!

So instead, little by little, we add in new stronger bricks to support the rotten crumbling ones. This takes a long time.

In the meantime, the child who lived with hunger does not have the necessary building block to feel hungry.

The child who learnt to smile as a response to pain, in order to appease scary adults, will continue to use their fake smile.

> **Our children need more than just secure foundations...**
> **They need the crumbling bricks to be replaced.**

2

Raising Penguins

I know our children frustrate us. They upset us, hurt us and sabotage the lovely things we do for them.

They are not nasty, spiteful children. They are in pain and fear and come at us from a place of trauma. Step back. Breathe. Imagine them at their emotional age, not their chronological one, and respond to them as the impulsive, scared children that the rest of the world doesn't see.

Traditional parenting models do not work, or they are only effective for a short time.

Blame is futile.

9

Penguins Don't Fly

(Our Children Are Different)

> My child is 11 now and really should be able to remember to put his washing away. It's really annoying that he doesn't. He needs to learn!

On a remote island there lived a pair of puffins. They were very happy but just wanted a baby puffin to care for and complete their family.

One day they came across an egg which had been abandoned. They nurtured the egg, kept it warm and hoped for the best.

Sure enough, soon a little black and white face peeped out and the baby bird made the family complete.

Everyone was very happy; things seemed to be going well. There was just one problem. While the baby was doing well with swimming, the flying was not so great. The puffin parents tried everything. Cajoling, encouraging, being angry and even threatening.

When the baby was a year old and still not flying, Dad puffin had had enough.

He took the baby up to the top of the cliff and said, 'Look, son, the only way you are going to learn to fly is if you really have to. You are one now and although the swimming is coming along great…birds must fly. It is expected and it's about time you started to fit in.'

'But I can't fly,' said the baby. 'I've tried and tried. My wings don't work.'

Daddy Puffin sighed and said, 'Don't worry, you will be fine.' He pushed the baby off the cliff. The baby didn't fly. He flapped and flapped his wings as hard as he could, but they just didn't work.

An older, wiser Puffin saw what had happened and said to Daddy Puffin, 'Why did you do that?'

The stricken father replied, 'I was trying to help him learn to fly.'

'Ah,' replied the wise puffin, 'but that was a penguin. Penguins cannot fly no matter how hard they try, but they are great swimmers.'

There is no reason why our children cannot achieve their true potential – as long as we respond to them in a way they can understand! Children who have suffered early life trauma have brains which have developed differently. They might see a threat where there is none; they may be *unable* to relax, concentrate or stop feeling anxious; they might be unable to remember simple routines.

We must not expect children who are struggling with these additional problems to be able to think and act as if they did *not* have these issues. It is up to us as the adults, parents, teachers, social workers and therapists to change *our* approach and expectations.

Traditional parenting models help to teach our 'birds to fly'. We are raising penguins. Don't throw your penguins off a cliff to try to make them fly!

10

The Messy Nest

(Destruction)

My child does not seem to appreciate the beautiful home we have created for her. We put so much thought and effort into her bedroom, but everything just gets destroyed or broken.

It's so important to create the right environment, fitting it to the child, not trying to make the child fit the new environment. After all, when birds create a nest for their fledglings, they are expecting them to be able to fly the nest one day...

As you decorate the nursery or bedroom, you might imagine how happy your child will be looking at the beautiful pictures on the wallpaper. That will surely help them to feel secure as they fall asleep.

As you shop for food that you think your child will like, you check that it's not too high in sugar. It needs to be wholesome and nutritious. You want your child to grow strong and healthy.

As you buy clothes for your child, you are careful to ensure that everything matches and it's of good quality. You want to feel proud of your child. You want others to comment on how well dressed she is. How beautiful.

Then your child arrives.

She is a penguin.

She cannot settle in the bedroom because there is no water in it. It's a frightening place. She flaps about and makes a bit of a mess. It's too hot. She hasn't had wallpaper before. She wonders what it tastes like. She did not mean to rip it. She wasn't thinking about that.

She cannot stand the food you have bought. There is no fish for a start. She stares at the food you put in front of her. She does not know what shepherd's pie is. It might be poisonous.

She didn't mean to reject you. She wasn't thinking about that.

When you give her the beautiful clothes, she is puzzled. Penguins don't wear clothes. They do not fit. The labels make her skin itch and she tries to pull them off. They rip.

She didn't mean to rip the clothes. She just needed to get them off.

The way she survived before was by swimming really fast in the open sea, but here there is only a tiny pool, called a bath.

You made a nest instead of a pool.

A child needs to recreate an environment they are familiar with. Penguins need pools.

11

The Girl Who Wouldn't Try

(Self-Sabotage)

I have tried using reward charts with my child, but this nearly always goes wrong. Why?

'Right', says Chloe's teacher. 'I have an exciting event for you all! Today we are going to go out onto the school field and play some games. I have this lovely chart here with a happy sun on the top and a sad cloud on the bottom. Everyone starts in the middle. All those of you who try really hard and do well will be moved onto the sun. Anyone who does not try or makes bad choices will move down towards the cloud. Everyone who is on the sun at the end of the games gets a reward. I expect everyone to do their best!'

The children go out excitedly onto the field. Chloe follows behind feeling unsure and a bit worried. She doesn't like change.

The first game is hopscotch. The teacher divides the children into teams and they all throw themselves into the game enthusiastically. Except Chloe. She sits at the side watching sadly. The teacher notices and, sure enough, Chloe's marker is moved down on the chart towards the sad cloud. Everyone else's goes up.

'You must try harder, Chloe,' says the teacher.

'But I can't do it,' replies Chloe.

The teacher sighs impatiently and says, 'You need to learn. You are eight years old now and you just need to join in a bit more.'

The next game is a short race. All the children get ready on the start line, then run as fast as they can.

Except Chloe.

Chloe stays on the start line.

The teacher is frustrated. She moves Chloe's marker down again, then goes up to her and says exasperatedly, 'What is it this time? You really must try to fit in a bit more!'

'The wheels on my wheelchair get stuck on the grass,' explains Chloe sadly.

'Oh *that* excuse again,' says the teacher angrily. She moves Chloe's marker straight to the sad cloud. 'Well, maybe that will help you to try a bit harder,' she says.

Where there is trauma, children's brains develop differently. We would not expect a child in a wheelchair to suddenly be able to get up and run a race. In the same way it is unreasonable to suddenly expect a child who interprets the world differently and is consumed by fear to put that fear and confusion to one side in order to conform to *our* reality.

It's not because I won't. It's because I *can't*.

12

Squeezing the Glass

(Over-Controlling)

My teenager is constantly going off out. It's getting worse and worse. He doesn't say where he is going. I am going to ground him for a month!

You have been bought a beautiful glass vase. It is very precious and special. Proudly, you put it on the shelf and admire it. It looks a bit dusty to you, so you take it down and polish it. You put it back on the shelf and go about your business.

You notice that your polishing has slightly worn part of the intricate pattern, so you make a mental note not to polish it too hard anymore.

You admire the vase sparkling on the shelf, but you have a niggling feeling that it really does need a bit more polishing. You can't help yourself. Even though you know you should really leave it alone, you keep polishing it. The lovely pattern starts to wear away.

The vase is very special to you and you worry that someone might accidentally knock it over. You start to move it around from room to room with you, just in case.

Your friend asks you what on earth you are doing walking about with the vase all the time. She asks to have a look at it. You are very worried and say she cannot look at it as she may wear the pattern off. She tries to persuade you to at least just put the vase on the shelf and leave it alone. She says you are being a bit controlling.

'It's *my* vase,' you say. 'It will go wherever I decide.'

Your friend decides to leave.

You sit holding your vase on your lap, thinking about what your friend has said. The pattern has worn off now. It does not look as beautiful. You hold the vase tight, worrying about what could happen to it if you leave it on the shelf. You squeeze the vase tighter and tighter.

It shatters into a million pieces, cutting your hands.

You held your precious vase too tightly.

When our children grow, we naturally fear for them. We try to hold them tighter, control them more. We are trying to keep them safe, but the tighter we hold them, the more we control, the faster they will run. It's so important to take stock of what you can, and cannot, control.

The harder we try to control, the more likely it is we will fail.

13

The King of the Castle

(Traditional Consequences Don't Work)

I have tried telling my child off, sending her to her room and removing toys to make her behave. Sometimes it seems to work briefly, but then we are back to square one!

The king sat in his castle. He was a powerful king and he liked to make sure he had control of everyone around him. He was very strict.

One of the king's servants was a peasant. He was very hungry. The peasant looked longingly at the mouth-watering bowls of fruit laid out in front of the king. Often the fruit would go off without being eaten. Sometimes, when no one was looking, the servant would quickly take a piece of fruit and eat it.

One day the king noticed the servant taking a piece of fruit.

'What!?' he roared. 'How dare you steal the royal fruit?' The king ordered that the servant spend seven days in prison as punishment.

When the servant came out of prison, he was even hungrier. He did not want to go back to prison but he could not risk taking the fruit. Instead, he went down to the kitchens where the bread was kept and carefully ate the centre of the rolls of bread, placing the rolls back, hoping no one would notice what he had done. Unfortunately, the cook saw him. She told the king.

The king was outraged. He spoke to the servant and said, 'What is your most precious possession?'

'I only have one possession,' said the servant. 'It is a cup my mother gave me.'

'Right,' said the king, 'I am confiscating that. You will see what it feels like to have things taken away.'

The king felt very pleased with himself. He was sure he had taught the servant a lesson.

A courtier, who had seen what had happened, was worried. He dared to ask the king, 'Sire, are you sure this is the right thing to do? Taking the servant's only possession might be really dreadful for him.'

'Fiddlesticks!' replied the king. 'My mother used to take things off me all the time. It never did me any harm.'

The courtier looked around at the glittering palace with all the amazing objects. He did not say anything.

The servant was very sad, but he was still hungry. He was angry with the king too and felt more determined to make sure he got his revenge. He started looking for the food he could take as well as a precious object he might be able to sell. He knew he would have to be even more careful this time.

The king had taught him to be very sneaky indeed.

When we punish our children, it is largely instinctive. It feels like a reward for us! The shouting can be quite cathartic. We get caught up in a cycle of punishments where we take away more and more, and yet it doesn't seem to change the behaviours.

You need to put your moral code on the shelf. Drop all ideas of 'winning'. Unrelated punishments don't make sense to children who interpret the world differently, and expect to have their things taken away.

They are driven by survival instincts, so they might comply with a series of punishments, but you won't facilitate change!

> **Punishment might get compliance, but you won't get change.**

14

Lie Tennis

(Lying)

My child lies all the time. Sometimes I can spend hours trying to make him admit the truth. It's so blatant too!

Mum and Toby come out on to the 'Tennis court of truth'. They face each other across the net. Mum looks wary. Toby looks defiant.

Mum serves the first ball.

'Have you put your washing away?'

Toby returns a lie ball swiftly, 'Yes I have. Stop going on.'

He's not fast enough for Mum. She makes a good return. The ball is just in. 'I will check.'

Toby easily returns, 'You never trust me.'

The ball is out.

Mum goes off the court to check Toby's washing. The washing has not been put away. It is in the exact place she left it.

Mum returns to the court feeling really angry. She serves. 'Why did you say you had put your washing away when you had not? That was a lie.'

Toby returns, 'I **did** put it away. Someone must have got it back out.'

Mum responds, 'That is a ridiculous thing to say!'

Toby returns the lie ball, 'No one ever believes me.'

Mum and Toby continue back and forth for an hour. Neither gives up or gives in. Both are getting tired. Mum is determined to make Toby admit the truth. She thinks that if she can get him to admit the truth, there will be a magical incident. The magical incident will mean Toby never lies again.

Dad enters the court and sees what is happening. He knows there cannot be a magical incident. He used to waste his time doing this too. He tells Mum to go and have a rest. Then he adjusts the net so it is much higher.

Toby serves, 'Mum is picking on me. She says I didn't put my washing away.'

The ball hits the net. Dad stands still, holding his racket.

'That's interesting,' he says.

Toby serves again. 'Well, I really did put my washing away and no one ever believes me.'

The ball hits the net again. Dad sits down to have a little rest. 'Tell me more,' he says. He starts to sing a little song.

Toby keeps serving lie balls, but they just keep hitting Dad's safety net. After a short while they decide to abandon the game and go and do something else instead.

When they go inside, Mum is astounded. 'How did you stop him lying?' she asks.

'Simple,' Dad says, 'I stopped asking him questions, and didn't return the lie ball.'

Trying to *prove* that you are right and the child is wrong does not promote any real learning. There is *no* magical incident following on from an admission of guilt. Just the invocation of shame. Children with experience of trauma might lie because there is a grain of truth in their story. They might mix up what has *happened* with what is *happening*. They may not be lying, yet not telling the truth either! They may be terrified of admitting the truth. It might be automatic lying.

We don't need to join in this game. As long as the child knows we know they are not telling the truth, we can raise the net, catch the lie balls and get on with our lives.

How do we stop children lying? – Stop asking them questions.
(Sonia Handlin-Martin, personal communication)

15

The Apprentice Who Wasn't Sorry

(Fake Apologies)

> Every time I make my child say sorry, I just feel she is manipulating me and doesn't really mean it.

The office apprentice started off really well. She seemed to complete all her deadlines and file all the paperwork correctly.

Two weeks later, the manager noticed that the apprentice's waste paper bin had some important documents in it. The documents should have been actioned a week earlier and filed. The apprentice had said she had done it. The manager was aghast!

'Why are those documents in your bin?' she asked.

'Oh!' said the apprentice, 'I thought it was ok to just chuck them.'

The manager thought the apprentice did not understand the gravity of the situation. (She did not realize that the secretary had already been all through this.) The manager explained all about data protection to the apprentice.

The manager said the apprentice 'should at least apologize'.

The apprentice was not sorry. She thought the manager was making a big fuss about nothing. After all, no one had died. The apprentice was very keen for the manager to stop talking to her so she could get back to messaging her friends.

She was very bored listening to the manager going on and on about data protection. She wanted the noise to stop. She got all the documents out of the bin and made a serious face while looking at them. She even managed to make her eyes water a bit.

The manager waited expectantly. The apprentice realized the only way she was going to make the manager shut up and go away was to say sorry. She also remembered that she had arranged to meet a friend for lunch and needed the manager to give her an extended lunch break.

The apprentice did her best sorry face and mumbled, 'Sorry, this won't happen again, but it was not actually my fault.'

The manager saw that the apprentice looked upset and she had at least apologized, so she said, 'We'll leave it at that for now, but please do not do this again.'

'Please could I have a little break as I am feeling a bit upset?' the apprentice asked.

The manager felt uneasy but agreed the apprentice could have an extended lunch break.

The next week, the manager found all the documents

the apprentice had promised to sort out, stuffed under the photocopier in an unlocked drawer.

The manager went to the apprentice and demanded an explanation. She was very cross.

The apprentice huffed and sighed quite a lot as the manager was becoming quite annoying now and making such a big deal about it. She decided to say sorry lots of times as that would probably work again. The manager said, 'You can't just keep saying sorry but keep repeating the same mistake! You need to put things right!' This was news to the apprentice. After all, it wasn't her fault and she had already said sorry.

Eventually the manager went away talking about 'further steps.' The apprentice was annoyed about the constant interruptions to her social life. She had a great idea to help stop this happening again. Carefully, she wrote out a sign on a piece of A4 paper. She stuck it on a card and added a stick so it was like a little banner.

The next morning, the manager went to the apprentice to check if she had actually done any work. As she approached the desk the apprentice held up her sign. It said, 'I'm sorry ok?' The apprentice was very pleased that she was able to continue messaging uninterrupted, while simultaneously meeting the manager's needs.

Trying to get an apology from a child from trauma is unlikely to end well! Often the child will give a 'fake apology' in order to make the parent (or questioning adult) be quiet.

As our children live in 'Now' they are focused on getting their needs met in the moment, and making sure that they stay safe.

We cannot force a genuine apology; instead we need to help our children put things right. A fake apology must be treated with caution.

A forced apology does not change a child's actions.

16

The Lift

(Unintended Consequences)

> My child is so nasty to me. She is always trying to upset me by spoiling things, being defiant, trying to control everything and running away. She knows it upsets me, but she just carries on.

Imagine you are in a lift. You are the only person in the lift and you are going up to the 50th floor.

You have a bad cramping sensation in your stomach and you just know that you are going to have to fart. As you are alone, this would normally not be a problem, but you are worried someone else might call the lift.

You continue upwards. The stomach cramp gets worse. You have no choice but to let it out.

Phew, the relief. The lift fills with a very nasty rancid smell, but you feel much better.

Then, horror of horrors, the lift pings and starts to slow. You are only at the 23rd floor. The doors slide open and a well-dressed man walks in and also presses the 50th floor button. As the door closes, you can see that he has smelled the dreadful stench. He coughs and looks at you accusingly.

You stare at the floor mortified.

You now have to continue up to the 50th floor in silence, in a dreadful smell which he knows you must have produced.

You consider saying something like, 'I wonder what that awful smell is.' But you know that is futile. You can see the man is trying not to breathe.

The man keeps looking at you accusingly. His eyes are watering.

You start to feel indignant. You could not help having a bad stomach. When you farted, you were alone!

You say to the man, 'I did not fart at you. I just farted. Alone. It's not my fault you walked into it.'

The man looks at you incredulously. He clearly still blames you.

Our children did not choose the life they have. They didn't choose to be:

hypervigilant
scared
unable to concentrate

angry
aggressive
bedwetters
sensitive
sad
abandoned
unable to feel hunger or pain effectively
terrified of school
forgetful.

They didn't choose it. But we chose them.

Our children aren't evil – they aren't doing it *to* us. Even though it might feel that way. They are just surviving.

> **They are not doing it *to* you. They are just doing it.**

3

Ignorance Is Not Bliss
The Unhelpful Others

Before I met my children...

I did not know about developmental trauma.

I did not know that children from trauma needed different parenting.

I did not know that other parents, friends and family would sit on the sidelines, in silent judgement.

I thought the professionals would understand our pain and challenges.

I thought when we really struggled, they would help.

Instead they said, 'But you chose to adopt. You must sort it out.'

I didn't know they didn't know the answers either.

I didn't know that they would be so scared about being asked for complicated answers which they couldn't provide, that they would withdraw and blame me instead.

I didn't know because I am just an adopter.

I am not magic.

17

The Goldfish

(Risk-Averse Practice)

Every time I raise an issue which needs resolving, the support team become obsessed with risks which are not even there! It's one giant back-covering exercise and my child's needs are lost within it!

A little boy has sensory issues and one of the things he does is head-bang. His parents are very worried about this.

They go to the doctor. The doctor suggests they get him a helmet and refers them to a social worker to help.

The parents get a nice lightweight cycle helmet.

The social worker says, 'No, that is not the correct helmet. He needs a better one.' She provides a much bigger, heavier helmet.

The helmet is so big it falls over his eyes. It is so heavy he can hardly lift his head. He walks about, but constantly bangs into things. He is frustrated. He gets angrier.

He no longer head-bangs as it is too hard.

The parents tell the social worker that their child has lots more injuries from bumping into things he cannot see. He is very frustrated and they feel their relationship has deteriorated as he can't even see them properly.

'Well,' she says, 'The main thing is he isn't head-banging anymore.'

The social worker then notices the parents have a new pet. It is a goldfish.

She says they need to do a 'safe pet assessment'.

The assessment for the goldfish is two pages long.

It has questions like:

- How does your pet react to new people?
- How does your pet show aggression?
- Where does your pet sleep?
- How will you prepare your pet for a child joining your family?

The parents say that they do not understand why they are wasting time, effort, paperwork and money processing a risk assessment on a goldfish when their son is really struggling, and sustaining injuries due to the latest risk-averse solution.

The social worker says, 'It's the law.'

The parents check the law but can see no reference to goldfish risk assessments or forcing children to wear big heavy helmets. They tell the social worker that it is *not* the law.

The social worker says. 'It's our policy.'

We have all lost our way. We are wasting our precious time over-compensating for risks which *do not exist*, and hanging these on outdated, risk-averse policies and procedures.

There are some risks we *cannot* foresee or plan for, and some which are not even a risk! The essential, central theme *must* be the need to attach and form relationships.

Doing risk assessments on goldfish will not make a child safer or more emotionally secure.

18

The Measuring Stick

(Judgement from Others)

Every week I hear other parents talking about their child's achievements. It makes me so angry when I hear this ill-disguised conceit. Somehow it seems to magnify my own child's struggles and lack of recognition from others.

Jane is a Therapeutic Parent; she is struggling to help her daughter, Alice, to stay calm, keep out of violent situations and stop sabotaging her life. Jane often celebrates little achievements with her daughter, like the day she was able to share something for the first time at age nine.

Catherine Jones is a 'perfect parent'. She does not seem to see Alice sharing as an achievement. She smiles at Jane condescendingly when Jane tells her the good news.

Last week Catherine Jones boasted that her daughter, Anya, had just been made a prefect. Although this was wonderful of course, Jane was a bit tired of hearing about how perfect Anya was. This was the 25th boasting story she had heard this month. She had also heard about Anya winning a national swimming gala and starting her own charity fun run to help a species of frog which was under threat.

After school one day, Catherine asks Jane if Alice would like to join Anya in the 'Save a frog fun run'. Jane looks at Catherine, wondering what on earth she is talking about. She cannot imagine a world where people have time and energy to think about fun runs or frogs, let alone a combination of the two. Jane is further distracted as she can see Alice is staring at Anya aggressively. She can hear Anya saying proudly, '…and then Mummy said as I am a prefect now it means I am the best girl in the class!'

Luckily a wise teacher sees what is going on. She rushes over with a large, old-fashioned wooden ruler. Jane is alarmed. Catherine pauses in her boasting to see what is happening.

'Ah,' says the teacher, placing the end of the ruler on the floor, 'let's just see if we have the right measurements.'

She measures Alice first and reads off, 'Has made great progress with sharing and having kind hands.'

Then she measures Anya. She reads off, 'Doing well with environment care but needs to be careful about showing off.'

The teacher then walks over to Catherine and Jane. 'We must be very careful,' she says, 'that we are using the right stick to measure children with.'

Jane is thrilled. She cannot resist holding the ruler against

Catherine's head and reading, 'Further measuring stick required to gauge correct height of boastfulness. Out of range.'

Therapeutic Parents do not try to 'keep up with the Joneses' because:

- they don't know who the Joneses are
- they don't care how great the Joneses' children are and how many awards they have won
- they are too busy regulating their children.

They just wish the Joneses would stop making all our children into a giant competition and instead help them out a bit!

Was kind to cat
Shared well
Did not wet bed

If you want to measure your child's achievements, be sure you are using the correct ruler.

19

The Cart

(Our Burden)

I feel so alone. I really thought that my friends, family and all the services would be helping me. Even my partner seems to making things harder! What can I do?

We might start off by skipping along happily. Maybe we are hand-in-hand with a partner, maybe we are alone. Either way, we are unencumbered when we start our journey.

Then we decide to have children. This might be through adoption or fostering or having birth children. We may anticipate that there might be some problems. We buy a nice, sturdy, heavy cart we can put the children in.

As the children arrive, we put them in the cart. We can't really skip along anymore because the cart is quite heavy. That's ok, we knew what we were getting into; we expected the cart to be heavy and we expected it to stop us running about and having fun all the time.

The path gets steeper. The cart gets heavier. You wonder why the cart is suddenly so heavy! You haven't looked behind you for a long time because you've just carried on putting one foot in front of the other and pulling the cart with all your might.

You stop to have a rest and look behind you at the cart. That's ok, the children are still sitting in the cart. But, oh no! There are other people in the cart too!

You did not expect your partner to be sitting in the cart as well. You thought they would be helping you, but you realize now you're the only one with the harness around you. Then, to your horror, you see the social worker, the teacher and even the GP, who have all attached themselves to the cart and are being dragged along behind it. This is obviously making the cart much heavier to pull and much more difficult.

You can also see that your best friend and your sister are attached to the cart by a thin rope and are trying to pull it back down the hill. You are amazed that you have managed to get this far entirely alone. You did not even realize you were alone!

You walk behind the cart and tell the social worker, GP and teacher that they had jolly well better start helping you to push the cart. After all, that is their job. They look a bit sheepish.

To your sister and best friend, you say, 'You can either help me push or I'm going to cut the rope that you're using to pull the cart back down the hill.' They look astonished.

Then you go to your partner and say, 'Get out of the cart right now and help me to get our children up this hill. I'm not pulling you along with them!' Your partner meekly gets out of the cart and starts helping you to pull the children. Suddenly the cart seems very light and you are making amazing progress.

Who knew that by losing some of the 'helpers' your load would lighten!

One of the main problems Therapeutic Parents share is that of feeling isolated. Often, they tell us that they feel they bear the load alone and are constantly having to fight to get the most basic resources and meaningful support.

Well, no shrinking violet ever changed the world! You need to review who is helping you and who is hindering you. Sort your cart out!

Remember to regularly check who is *in* your cart and who is helping you.

20

The Ostrich Teacher

(Unhelpful Schools)

My child always has loads of homework to do. I've tried explaining to the school that she really struggles and it takes up all our time and creates lots of conflict, but they just say she has to do it!

It's really difficult having an ostrich for a teacher!

I've been in to see my child's teacher every day this week to talk about all the problems we are having.

The Ostrich Teacher thinks that because he learnt about reward charts when he was training, that is the only way forward. I've explained that when he uses reward charts with my child she is catapulted into shame, but the Ostrich Teacher turns around and puts his head in the sand pit.

Then there is the homework. Every time we sit at home and try to do the homework it creates so much conflict and stress. I can't get on with my life, and everything my child remembered yesterday she doesn't remember today! When I spoke to the Ostrich Teacher about this, he just said, 'All children have to do homework and the school expects it.' And then he turned round and put his head in the sand again!

I've given the Ostrich Teacher lots of material about how trauma affects children, the way they think and the way they learn. He hasn't even picked it up off his desk!

This week I had an idea. I invited the Ostrich Teacher out into the playground where there was no sand at all, just concrete. I explained that my child cannot cope with me changing roles from 'mum' to 'teacher'. I told him that if he wanted us to do homework that was fine, but he would need to come round and supervise my child tidying her bedroom. After all we are not expecting school to do our job, so I don't know why school is expecting us to do theirs!

The Ostrich Teacher looked a bit worried when he realized he was standing on concrete.

I said, 'You can carry on burying your head in the sand if you want, but there is a whole tsunami of knowledge and change coming up behind you, about how we educate children from trauma.'

The Ostrich Teacher frantically banged his head on the concrete, knocking himself out.

We don't do homework anymore.

School stays at school! Your job is hugely important. You are working on your child's attachment; their interpretation of the world; their ability to trust. If we cannot get those fundamentals in place, then knowing the 4-times table is not going to help your child to survive in our world.

Leave homework for school. You have more important things you need to achieve!

21

The Snowflake Parent

(Unhelpful Others)

I always try really hard to use empathy when I respond to my child. My friends laugh at me and say I am a 'snowflake parent'.

Therapeutic Parents need to parent a different way.

Snowflakes are all individual. No two are the same.

Therapeutic Parents often really worry about getting it wrong and what people might think.

Snowflakes are beautiful and perfect.

Therapeutic Parents have a long and tricky road ahead. They have not chosen an easy route through life.

Snowflakes have travelled great distances and overcome insurmountable odds just to arrive at their destination.

Therapeutic Parents just keep on keeping on with calm perseverance. Every day brings a challenge, and every day they worry about their child's future and if they will ever even get them to their destination.

Snowflakes always settle somewhere. Quietly, without a fanfare.

Therapeutic Parents often feel alone and isolated. Sometimes they feel they are the only person dealing with the issues they face. They find others in the same situation. They join their voices together.

Snowflakes join the other snowflakes. They merge together to make a formidable force. Transforming the world into a beautiful place.

Often it can feel very overwhelming to hear criticism from others who do not understand how parenting children from trauma is different. Your friends and relatives may not understand the power of empathy and the strong connections it builds, and the way it heals your child.

That's ok. You don't need to justify your parenting to them. It is sad that they are not educated. Lend them some books on the subject.

Then go right back to doing exactly what you know you need to do for your child.

Completely put aside society's expectations for your child's achievements, and for their behaviour developmental stage. That is for ordinary birds. Remember your bird is a penguin. Your penguin will learn to swim in her own time and in her own way. The most important thing is for her to know you understand her, support her and have her back.

Never underestimate a snowflake.

4

Parenting in the Trauma Tornado

Children can come through most events if they have a safe and reliable point of reference. An 'unassailable safe base'. Structure, routine and boundaries are *the* most important parts of Therapeutic Parenting.

Children need to be able to rely on a reliable, warm parent and be able to take cues from them to make sense of their world.

Most of all, children need to know where they stand, where the boundaries are and that they are loved and accepted.

Therapeutic Parents walk at their own PACE.[1] They are undeterred and work hard not to be distracted by the chaotic events surrounding them.

---

1   PACE is an acronym created by Dan Hughes and stands for Playfulness, Acceptance, Curiosity and Empathy. This is widely used within Therapeutic Parenting techniques. (D. Hughes (2009) *Attachment-Focused Parenting.* New York: W.W. Norton.)

22

The Eye of the Storm

(Managing Chaos)

> My life is chaos! There is one problem after another.
> Damage, anger, relentless madness. I am exhausted.

Imagine a tornado. You might have one in your own home. What is in your trauma tornado? Maybe you hear screeches, screams, arguing and fighting...

'I've lost my shoes! You stole them!'
'Hurry up, we HAVE to leave!'
'Noooooooooo!!! I hate you!!'
'Fat pig, I wish you died!'

You might see mess, damage, chaos, everything in the wrong place...

new scrape marks on the sideboard
another chair that has lost a leg
another door with a hole in it
children deliberately hurting each other
remote control... Lost, never to be seen again.

You might smell...

urine from the beds and in other random places
faeces – everywhere!
body odour from sweaty children refusing to wash
rotting food from under beds, school bags and other hiding
    places.

The Trauma Tornado is not a nice place to live in.

So, we must create a safe space within it. A space we can parent in.

Every storm has a centre and at the centre is calm. The Therapeutic Parent places themselves at the centre of the storm, seeing the chaos but not joining it. Breathe, observe and pause before acting.

The Therapeutic Parent aims to be the calm in the centre of the Trauma Tornado.

23

The Elephant

(Staying Kind)

'Choose your battles wisely,' they say. Well, try doing that when he's deliberately winding me up every minute of every day! It's very hot today and he won't even let me apply sunscreen. He's ruining the day for us all. I just can't seem to let things bounce off me.

The elephants were having a lovely time splashing around in the water. The little elephant was in a very bad mood. He pushed and prodded his mother with his head. His mother acknowledged he was having a difficult day but still he pushed and prodded.

Mummy elephant felt it was best to end the lovely swamp bath early and to go for a nice long walk instead. Maybe this would settle the little elephant.

As he walked behind her, he gathered rocks in his trunk and hurled them at her, one after another, in quick succession. His mother knew exactly what was happening, but her skin was so thick she couldn't feel the rocks hitting her. They just bounced off.

The little elephant wondered why his mum wasn't getting cross.

'I know,' he thought, 'I will throw a whole handful of rocks really close. That will get her attention!' He picked up a big pile with his trunk.

He called his mum 'Oi! Come back here! Why aren't you getting angry?' he shouted at her.

The mother elephant turned to the little elephant. Just below her chest he saw a great big heart-shaped marshmallow.

The little elephant was furious. He quickly threw all the rocks with all his might. They went straight into the pink marshmallow heart and got stuck there. He tried to pull them out again but he couldn't.

'Oh dear,' said his mother. 'It looks like your angry stones made my heart get bigger.'

It is important that we develop a thick skin when caring for children who display consistently annoying behaviours. We need to let some things bounce off us or we will quickly become exhausted and our empathy cup will empty.

Keeping an open and soft heart towards our children can be very difficult when the behaviours are relentless, but it's imperative that we do.

Therapeutic Parents need a skin like an elephant and a heart like a marshmallow.

24

The Steam Train

(Keeping on Track)

> I find I am often side-tracked by my child. I might be trying to leave the house or get her to bed, but she distracts me with new issues!

The Therapeutic Parent Steam Train is a formidable train. It just keeps going no matter what! Your train might have any number of carriages. One, two, or even seven or eight!

We are on the track and we know where we are heading: Secure Attachment Station.

Our little carriages do not understand that we know what we are doing and where we are going. They have their own ideas and want to follow a different track. That track leads to Chaos. The carriages know all about Chaos, as that's often the station they started from. Chaos is a pretty horrible place, but the carriages are familiar with it.

On our journey, we might stop at lovely stations along the way. They have nice cafés which gave the carriages some nurture. Sometimes the Steam Train just stops and lets everyone rest for a while and catch their breath. Very often, the little carriages are able to leave some of their heavy baggage at these stations. Baggage they no longer need.

After stopping for one of these rests, one of the carriages does not want to follow the Steam Train. The carriage thinks the Steam Train cannot be trusted to go the right way. The Steam Train has said it is time to go. The little carriage tries its best to jump onto a different track, but as the Steam Train keeps moving forwards the carriage falls quickly in behind.

It's hard work heading to Secure Attachment Station all the time! The Steam Train needs lots of coal to power the engine. There are some great drivers who provide special coal. The best kind is coal from Empathy and Understanding Ltd. It makes the Steam Train's task much easier. Some drivers are not so great at keeping the fire going. Sometimes they are a bit distracted by the noise the carriages are making. They occasionally use special water from Blame and Judgement Ltd to dampen the fire down and make the Steam Train's job even harder,

It is so easy for our children to distract us down a road we did not mean to go! This happens especially at transitions, like bedtimes. Suddenly some earth-shattering statement needs to be heard, or a big drama happens, which apparently only you can resolve. Keep in mind what you are trying to achieve, stay on track and remind your child of what they need to do.

Your children are skilled at showcasing what they want, but this is almost never what they need!

What your children *need* is different to what they *want*. The Therapeutic Parent Steam Train keeps everyone on track.

25

The Rude Wind

(Responding to Rudeness)

How can I stop my child being so rude to me? I tell him off but that seems to make it worse!

The cedar tree thought the wind was very rude. It constantly blew at her and buffeted her, generally trying to be irritating. The noise from the wind was constant. The cedar tree would wave its branches and tell the wind to go away. The wind just laughed at her and called her rude names.

'You are a big fat tree! Ha ha! You can't get me! I can go wherever I want, but it's fun just annoying you!'

The cedar tree tried all kinds of threats. She puffed herself out and made herself bigger and bigger. She made more and more threats.

'If you carry on this way, you are going to regret it. How dare you be so rude?!'

It seemed that the angrier the cedar tree became, the more the rude wind blew. The rude wind was thrilled that the cedar tree had puffed herself out so much. Now he had a much bigger target!

Next to the cedar tree was a willow tree. The willow tree also thought the wind was very rude, especially when the rude wind sent a sudden, unexpected gust in the middle of the night.

'Ha ha!' the rude wind mocked the willow tree, 'You can't get me, you're an idiot!'

The willow tree felt the rude wind going through his branches and moved softly with the breeze. The willow tree started singing a soft lullaby.

The rude wind was very annoyed that he hadn't made the willow tree angry, so he tried again. 'Stupid fat idiot! Stop singing, it's hurting my ears!'

The cedar tree heard what was happening and got more and more angry. She started threatening the wind with all kinds of punishments. She said she would call a meeting of all the trees in the woods and get the rude wind banished. The rude wind became very upset about this and blew with all his might. He suddenly found he had lots of energy, and the rude wind became a frightening gale.

The cedar tree, so large and puffed out, was uprooted and came crashing down.

The willow bent with the gale and, afterwards returned to his usual position.

The rude wind was mortified. He had not understood the power of his own strength.

The beautiful cedar tree lay on the ground. As she faded away, she asked, 'Where did I go wrong?'

'You never learned how to let the rude wind blow through you, so you could stay strong,' replied the willow.

Sometimes we parents can find ourselves getting more and more stuck in confrontation.

An onslaught of rudeness or lying might be met with 'How dare you! Apologize right now! You are not going anywhere!', etc.

We can stand strong, allow 'the rude wind' to pass through us and then go harmlessly out the other side.

The bigger the target, the more likely the fall – think willow!

26

The Conductor

(Controlling Behaviour)

My child is such a manipulator! No one else seems to see it. She often says and does things to control people but they don't realize. When I tell them, they just think I am a nasty parent! What can I do?

The survivor conductor is a very skilled individual. They have had to be.

The way they survive is to make sure they can see everything that is going on at all times and that they remain in charge.

Hold on! It looks like the violinist is getting on very well with the trombonist. They are having a lovely chat.

The conductor is very worried. They have forgotten about her. She is invisible. They cannot keep time with the music. Everything is going wrong!

The conductor tells the trombonist that she heard the violinist saying nasty things about them. The trombonist is horrified. He thought the violinist was his friend. He stops talking to the violinist.

The conductor happily continues conducting.

Wait a moment! The cellist is not even looking at the conductor. She feels all wobbly. What if the cellist forgets about her? What if she is left alone in an empty, dark orchestra pit? What if the music stops?

The conductor feels so wobbly it seems that her baton might accidentally slide out of her hands. The baton hits the cellist across the cheek and leaves a red mark.

The cellist is furious.

The conductor says it was not her fault. It was the baton.

The orchestra manager comes out to see what all the noise is about.

There is lots of shouting and pointing.

The conductor says, 'This is only my second time conducting. I thought they would all be here to support me but they aren't.'

The orchestra manager looks a bit unsure. Seeing this, the conductor frantically continues, 'They are all bullying me! They won't do what I say.'

The conductor bursts into tears.

The orchestra manager is convinced and starts to tell the orchestra off.

'Excuse me,' says a voice from the stalls. 'I was sitting in the audience, behind the conductor. I saw everything.'

'And who might you be?' asks the orchestra manager.

'I am a Therapeutic Parent,' says the man.

Children who have experienced trauma are frightened of being forgotten. If they are not at the centre of everyone's thoughts, they are unimportant. They might starve. They will be very sad and lonely.

So, automatically the orchestra is conducted to ensure the child stays the focal point. Our job is to stand behind the child, observe what they are doing and let them know we know, *without* dancing to the tune.

In order to see what is *really* going on, stand behind the conductor of the orchestra.

27

The Missiles

(Responding to Arguing)

My child argues with me all the time. No matter what I say, they just seem to twist it. Everything is all about them!

Imagine a spaceship, The TP1 is piloted by defenders of the Earth, patrolling the skies to keep us all safe. The crew are wise and creative people.

One day they see a small alien spacecraft approaching. TP1 sends out a friendly, enquiring message:

'Greetings! You are entering Earth Space. How can we assist you?'

The alien craft responds with silence.

TP1 tries again in a different language. No response.

TP1 says, 'You must respond or withdraw.'

The alien spacecraft sends a missile towards TP1. Although the forcefield easily deals with the missile, TP1 is now on full alert.

TP1 goes into 'Full Defence Mode' and launches its own missile. As the missile hits the alien craft, it does not appear to damage it in any way.

The alien craft fires a larger, more powerful missile. This one dents TP1's forcefield. TP1 immediately returns fire with several powerful missiles.

Almost before their eyes, the crew of TP1 see the alien craft growing stronger. It seems to absorb the power from TP1's missiles!

Captain Pace realizes what is happening.

'The alien craft is gathering energy from *our* missiles and using it to fire back at us. The more we respond, the more powerful they will grow! Cease fire!'

TP1 stops firing and watches. The next missiles from the alien craft are much smaller. They do not dent the forcefield. As the crew watches, the alien craft becomes weaker and smaller. Soon it is smaller than when they first saw it.

Suddenly the alien craft leaves, almost with a flounce.

How do we stop our children arguing? Stop arguing! Yes, I did have a child who could argue with herself, but that's fine, the missiles did not get through my forcefield.

When we join our children in arguments, we are simply donating ammunition.

28

The Cliff Top

(Keeping Boundaries)

I try not to worry too much about boundaries and routine as I like to be flexible and reactive. Surely it doesn't really matter?

Imagine that you have to walk along the top of a cliff. You can see the sea crashing below and the wind is blowing quite strongly. The cliff top goes in and out and it doesn't look at all safe to you as a part is crumbling away. You think this is a really stupid idea and you just want to go home and have a cup of tea.

Unfortunately, however, you have to do this because you must get to your destination. The only way to get to where you need to be is to walk along this cliff top, so you have no choice.

You look behind you in a last desperate attempt to see if you can go back the way you came but you cannot; that part is now blocked. You look around for somebody to help you. You also look to see far ahead if there is any kind of fence along the cliff top. That would make you feel a lot better as the path is quite narrow.

There is no fence.

You stand there a long time. You don't know where the edges are as it is quite dark now.

Suddenly a man approaches you. He says, 'Right, let me just slip this on you and then we can start our journey.' He has a blindfold.

Now you are shaking with terror. You can't see any way that you're going to get to where you need to be safely. You are likely to die in the process. You start shouting and swearing at the man. Is he some kind of idiot? How much more difficult could this be?!

You have no choice but to put the blindfold on and start walking along the cliff edge. You start trying to feel your way with your feet. It's not possible and so you just freeze in terror, sit down on the grass and stay put. At least this way you won't die.

A lady called Liza comes up to you. She holds your hand and says, 'It's ok, I don't have a blindfold on. I can see where we are going. I have a torch too. You can walk next to me. I will walk alongside the cliff edge, and you can stay on my right, away from the cliff top. That way we can both get to the destination together safely. Just make sure you do not go past my boundary.'

You start walking along together. At first you are constantly close to falling off the cliff top. But Liza just keeps walking. Keeping you on her right and reminding you each time you stray too far.

When you finally reach your destination, you realize that you can take off your blindfold and clearly see your own way.

Often our children have had a very difficult start in life and are unsure about what is and is not ok. Suddenly they are plopped on top of a new cliff top, with no idea about what the rules are. It can feel like trying to navigate the top of a cliff blindfolded!

It is tempting to overcompensate and 'make allowances', but this misplaced empathy can lead to *unsafe* parenting. Unsafe parenting might include the avoidance of expressed anger or a failure to reinforce boundaries; in turn, this can allow children to 'fall off the cliff' by permitting without challenge violence, aggression, rudeness, conflict and extreme behaviours.

Therapeutic Parenting *does not* do this! Our children *need* us to be the unassailable safe base. To be strong through instruction and direction about where the boundaries are, and to be clear with them about what is, and is *not* ok.

Our children often behave in unacceptable ways. It is our job to steer them, using clear direction and strong boundaries.

29

The Inquiry Lie

(Honesty)

My child has a very difficult early history. The social worker has said we should tell her that her parents 'couldn't look after her properly', but it's so much worse than that! How do I protect her?

Today they published the results of the inquiry into the worst plane crash of all time. The plane crash killed 576 people. Five passengers and the pilot survived.

The government have said that there was an oversight when the mechanic signed off the plane. The report said that he won't do it again and he didn't really mean it, so we should all forget about it and move on and try not to blame him.

Five-hundred and seventy-six people are dead.

As well as the mechanic not doing his job, the pilot was drunk. If the pilot had not been drunk, he could have seen the mistake that the mechanic made and he could have sorted it out. He didn't notice the mistake.

The government said that the pilot is very sorry. He has said he won't drink anymore and therefore we should not blame him, but try to understand that he was going through a very tricky time.

Five-hundred and seventy-six people are dead.

The survivors and relatives of the people who died are very angry indeed! They have demanded that the government hold people to account and tell them the truth.

The government say they have told the truth! They have narrowed the problem down to an oversight by the mechanic and a lapse in judgement by the pilot. The pilot is still flying planes; the mechanic is still mending planes. The government say it is hard to get people with their skills so they don't want to fire them. They have definitely been told off though.

Five-hundred and seventy-six people are dead.

The survivors and relatives are outraged. How can this be? What version of the truth is this?

They know that, at best, the government are being economical with the truth. After all, the survivors remembered what happened. They were there! They know the truth, but they cannot prove it.

They have lost all trust in the government and are stuck in a place of fear, dread and anger. They can no longer trust anybody, and they certainly will not be flying again.

Children know the truth of what happened to them. No matter how difficult the story is, it is important to be honest and straightforward. Anything else is short-changing our children. We can join them in their bewilderment and grief, and absolve them of any portion or sense of blame. In doing so, we remain firmly on the child's side and identify ourselves as a person to be trusted.

Although it is tempting to water down unpalatable truths, this is received by children as a lie, and makes it harder for them to trust.

Be careful not to water down unpalatable truths so far that you leave your child drowning.

5

SAFER Parenting
Therapeutic Responding

Now we have established how important structure, routine and boundaries are, how can we best respond to our children in a way which will help them?

It's difficult to put our own stresses and emotional responses to one side, but one of the best ways to use Therapeutic Parenting is to think carefully about what you are seeing, try and work out what the behaviour is telling you, and respond with empathy.

We call this SAFER Parenting:

Secure
Attachments
From
Empathic
Reparenting

30

The Needle on the Record

(Changing Our Responses)

> My child keeps on asking nonsense questions! I've tried ignoring him, but it doesn't make any difference. In fact it gets worse!'

When I was a child, I had a record player. Sometimes the record would get scratched and the needle would stay stuck, going round and round, repeating the same scratched section of the song.

I got angry with the record player. I told it off. That did not work.

I complained to my parents. 'The stupid record player keeps getting stuck!' My parents told me to jog the record player. I thought they were being stupid.

I went back and shouted at the record player, but it stayed stuck.

It didn't matter how much I huffed, sighed, shouted and complained, the record kept going round and round. Stuck.

I needed to interact in a different way to make the change happen and get the result I wanted.

In frustration I banged the record player. The needle jumped and moved out of the scratch. Well, who would have thought it? My parents had been right.

I quickly learnt that I had to jog the record player to jump the needle out of the groove. Then the song would keep playing until it got stuck on the next scratch.

Giving the child the same response to entrenched behaviours is not going to change anything. We will all just keep going round and round in circles!

We must change our response to our children's stuck behaviours in order to make the changes we need!

It's too easy to get stuck in a useless cycle of blame, punishment and victim mentality. We are not the victims, and our children do not need to remain or become victims either.

Changing our response is the best way to change the behaviour.

31

The Plane Crash Part 2

(Unable to Calm)

> My child cannot seem to calm down. I have tried sending her to her room until the tantrum stops but it seems to make it worse!

In Chapter 5 (The Plane Crash Part 1) our poor passenger had a dreadful time. No one seemed to understand or help them! We are not very lucky with planes. They always seem to be crashing. This time we have a different outcome though!

Imagine you are sitting on a plane, doing a crossword puzzle. Suddenly you hear a loud bang. You look out of the window and see an engine is on fire. There is panic! You throw the crossword puzzle down and start frantically looking around to see what the cabin crew are doing.

You are slightly reassured to see that although they are busy, and clearly aware of the problem, they are showing no signs of panic.

The cabin crew move confidently and quickly through the cabin, reassuring people and making sure they are buckled in.

It's no good though. You can feel the panic rising higher and higher. When the cabin steward gets to you, you grab at him desperately and start screaming. You really believe you are going to die. You can't let go of his hand. You start crying. The other passengers around you start staring and looking worried too. An elderly lady is also crying and screaming hysterically, but the cabin crew are too busy and ignore her.

The cabin steward crouches down next to your seat. He explains very slowly and carefully that there is no real danger. The pilot has everything under control and the plane can fly safely on three other engines. The fire is out in the damaged engine.

You cannot believe it and keep crying and gripping his hand. The steward just stays near you, looking calm. Meanwhile, the elderly lady is bundled into the toilet and told to stay there until she can calm down. There are screaming and banging noises coming from the toilet. Everyone looks worried.

After a short while, you realize that the steward is indeed showing no signs whatsoever of panic or worry. He has even had a little joke with another passenger. Gradually you feel your pulse rate slow and you feel you are able to think straight.

Once the steward is sure you are ok, he leaves to get you a cup of tea.

You know it will be a while before you can pick up your

crossword puzzle again, but at least now you can breathe easily again. Meanwhile, you can still hear the screaming and banging noises coming from the toilet. Everyone has forgotten about the elderly lady. She can't see that everyone is calm and things are ok now. She gets louder and more hysterical.

You speak to the other cabin steward who put her in the toilet, 'Don't' you think you should let that poor lady out? She is getting more and more scared!'

'No,' says the steward. 'She has to learn. Once she is quiet, I will let her out. I can't have her disrupting the whole plane.'

You wonder how she can learn when she is terrified.

If someone tells you to 'calm down', do you immediately feel calmer and think 'Silly me?' Or do you fantasize about punching them in the face?

Telling someone to calm down, or removing a child and expecting them to be able to 'calm themselves down', simply increases fear. We need to stay close to our children and show them that their rage and fear does not control or faze us.

Parental presence is the key to calm.

32

ACE Detective

(Working Out What Is Behind the Behaviour)

> My child keeps on running off and hiding from me. I get really annoyed and he knows that, but he still keeps doing it! It feels like Groundhog Day! What can I do?

Every day it was the same! I would turn up at the school and Lewis would be hiding somewhere. It was very embarrassing and I had reached the end of my tether. I was sure he was doing it just to annoy me.

So one day I bought an amazing new gadget, the BrainCam, which would help me see inside his head. The next time he hid from me I was able to point the BrainCam at his head and watch a movie play, showing me what was going on in his mind at the time.

I was amazed to see that in his movie, when he was hiding, he was seeing a scary looking woman; she was walking into his room and she looked drunk. Lewis looked scared.

Then the movie changed and she was walking into his room very angry and shouting.

In the next part of the movie she was coming into his room and she looked fine, happy and calm, holding sweets for him. The woman was shouting at Lewis to come out.

In the next part, she was sitting in his room with a vacant expression on her face.

In all the movie clips Lewis was looking terrified, and he was hiding.

It was really useful to see this movie because I realized that he was hiding in order to check out that I had stayed the same. All I had to do was go to meet him, be my normal self and chat away in a relaxed way. Then he would come out of his hiding place and I could reassure him.

Once I worked out why he was doing it, I could sort it out. I think every parent should have one of these BrainCams!

Sadly, we cannot have BrainCams yet! But I am an ACE Detective. I don't mean a brilliant one (although I think I am sometimes); I mean an Adverse Childhood Experiences Detective. What does that mean? Well, whenever I see a behaviour *now*, I pretend my child is much younger. I see the world through their eyes and imagine what might have happened to cause this.

Sometimes I have to use a magnifying glass and mull things over really carefully.

Sometimes I need to read files or ask questions about their early life.

Sometimes I need to trust my instinct and go with that. It's nearly always right!

If we don't understand *where* a behaviour might have come from, we cannot know *how* to respond to change that behaviour.

33

The Frightened Dog

(Connecting in a Crisis)

> When my child is out of control, it doesn't matter what I do, he doesn't listen to me. What can I do differently?

The dog had got out of its kennel. He was terrified, he did not know where he was, and the traffic was really noisy.

He ran towards the road and became more scared. The owner saw the dog had got out and ran after him. He shouted at the dog, 'Get back here right now!' The owner was terrified. The dog was terrified.

The dog was trying to avoid cars whizzing close by, making the animal terrified. Would it be helpful for the owner to shout at the dog? To tell him off? To punish him afterwards for getting out by shutting him in a kennel? Would that action make the dog think, 'Hmm I see what I did wrong there. I ran in the road, and got really scared. So, fair enough I need to be locked in here alone now.'

Obviously not.

The owner needed to try to stop the traffic so that the dog was not in danger and stopped running about. He needed to recognize the dog's terror and to be careful on his approach and be aware that the dog was not his usual self and might bite him, out of character and from his place of terror. He needed to speak quietly and calmly. Making no sudden movements.

Once the owner was calm, the dog could approach him, receive comfort from him and perhaps accept a stroke or a treat.

The change in our behaviour towards a frightened animal is largely instinctual, and yet with a child it seems much harder.

We do not shout at the dog running in the road. We stop the traffic.

Even in a crisis, we need to recognize the feelings within the child and respond to those feelings, not the actions we are seeing. Instead of looking at what's happening on the surface, we need to recognize the underlying feelings and connect to the child at that point. This cuts through a lot of anger and facilitates change much faster.

Therapeutic Parents change:

- see
- think
- act

to:

- hear
- feel
- respond.

By responding to overwhelming feelings with calm and empathy, we reassure and regulate the child.

34

Sharing the PIE

(Sibling Rivalry)

I wish the children would stop vying for my attention all of the time and arguing over the most trivial things. They are acting like toddlers. They can't even share and are meant to be siblings for goodness sake!

Jenny is very anxious as Mum cuts a lovely homemade pie into pieces – one slice for each of the five children. Jenny shouts at Mum, demanding to have the biggest piece. She won't leave her side, not even for a moment. She is terrified that the others will get more pie than her or that she won't get any pie at all.

No matter how often Mum tries to reassure her that everyone gets an equal slice of the pie in this house, Jenny just won't listen. Mum desperately needs to use the toilet, and even though she is gone for just a few minutes, a fight ensues. Mum hears all the screaming and shouting and returns to find the children fighting over the pie. Jenny started the fight this time, but Mum doesn't realize this as Jenny is telling off all the other children for fighting.

Sadly, the pie is now just a big mess on the floor and the children begin to blame each other.

Mum is very cross and storms out of the room, stating that no one will get any pie if they don't start behaving properly and stop fighting. Jenny follows Mum into the kitchen and says sorry in a very matter-of-fact way.

Mum thanks Jenny for trying to stop the fight and offers her a small individual pie she made earlier for Jenny to eat on her own after the others have gone to bed.

All the children have to make do with oven chips and chicken nuggets – that's ok as they're quite accustomed to such foods, but they are a bit sad that it's not pie.

Jenny makes sure that the other children know that she had a pie all to herself after they had gone to bed. She doesn't tell them until the next morning.

Unfortunately, this starts yet another fight and another and another throughout the day.

What if we swap PIE for Parental Interaction Engagement!? What if that is what the children are really fighting for?

Siblings who have experienced trauma will recreate relationship dynamics which enabled them to *survive* in an environment where they were often overlooked, their needs unmet.

The children vie for your attention so they are not forgotten. They must be the best, the loudest, the strongest, the most favoured one. That will help them stay alive for sure! It's the only way they know.

Children will vie for PIE, as without PIE they die. PIE is Parental Interaction Engagement.

35

The Shame Pit

(Overwhelming Shame)

My child will never make a choice about anything. It doesn't matter how easy I make it. It's so annoying!

The man had two sandwiches on the plate. He asked Ben, 'Do you want a jam sandwich or a ham sandwich for your tea?'

Ben looked at the sandwiches and thought, 'Well, I quite fancy the jam sandwich,' so he said, 'I'll have a jam sandwich please.'

'Well that's not a surprise,' said the man, ' I thought you would choose something that was sweet because you're quite greedy about sweet things aren't you?'

The man threw the jam sandwich carelessly at Ben. Ben looked at the sandwich. He didn't really want it now. He felt a bit ashamed. He looked down at his feet and saw that the floor was a bit soggy. His feet were in the Shame Pit. It was not comfortable.

The next day the same thing happened. The man asked Ben, 'Do you want the jam sandwich or the ham sandwich?'

Ben thought, 'I'm not going to get caught out like that again!' He said, 'I'll have the ham sandwich, please.'

The man carelessly threw him a ham sandwich and said, 'I thought you would choose that. You like eating dead animals don't you? You don't even care about animals!'

Ben did not want a sandwich anymore. He looked down and realized he could no longer see his feet as he had sunk into the Shame Pit nearly up to his knees.

The next day the man presented Ben with the same two sandwiches. Ben was still in the Shame Pit and felt a bit wobbly. 'Which sandwiches would you like today?' asked the man.

Ben said he was not hungry. The man said, 'Come on, I know you're hungry, you need to choose one of the sandwiches.'

Ben knew that whatever sandwich he chose, it would be wrong. He did not want the man to know his thoughts, and so he said, 'I think I would like both of them please.'

The adult took the sandwiches away and said, 'Because you are so greedy, you get nothing.'

Ben realized the Shame Pit was up to his chest. He couldn't see a way out.

After that Ben never chose again. He knew that whatever he chose he would be judged for it and that he would end up sinking in the Shame Pit.

Our children often struggle to make choices because they are frightened of revealing their true thoughts and feelings. Their past experiences have taught them that each time they do they will pay. They are overwhelmed with shame which is often attached to choices they make. Surely it's easier to say nothing?

We can help them to climb out of the Shame Pit and risk making choices by avoiding questions and remaining neutral about their choices.

Where there is a big decision or someone else has had to ask a big question, preempt the fear: 'We have an important choice to make together and whatever we decide, I will still love you/feel the same way about you, and tea will still be at 5:30.'

Sometimes you need to put a ladder down the Shame Pit to help your child to climb out.

36

The Escalator

(Natural and Logical Consequences)

How can I allow my child to link cause and effect?

Sabotaging natural consequences

Rosie was out with her mum shopping. Shopping was really boring, so she thought she'd find something more interesting to do instead.

As they went towards the escalator, Rosie noticed a shiny red button. Underneath it said 'Emergency'. Rosie thought it would be really good fun to press it to see what would happen. She pressed the big red button and the escalator stopped dead. Rosie's mum turned to her aghast asking, 'Why did you do that?!'

Rosie said nothing. She just smiled happily at all the fuss.

Rosie's Mum sighed and said, 'Well, we will have to get the lift now.' Rosie was pleased. She liked the lift.

Natural consequences

The next time they were at the shopping centre, Rosie pressed the button again! Rosie's mum was mortified and very cross. She said, 'Oh well, that's a shame for you. We will have to stand here now and wait for the man to come and reset it.'

It was boring waiting for the man. Rosie wanted to go in the lift, but her mum just kept saying the bags were all too heavy.

The man came along quite quickly and reset the escalator, so Rosie and her mum moved towards it to go up the escalator. Rosie had got very bored waiting and she fancied a bit of excitement. She did not really fancy another long boring wait but she just could not help herself. Her hand was itching to press the tempting button.

Rosie pressed the big red shiny button and once again the escalator ground to a halt.

Rosie's mum was furious. She was also really embarrassed. All the people around were staring at them angrily.

'What on earth are you doing!?' She shouted at Rosie.

Rosie didn't say anything, but she did feel a bit worried that they might have to wait around a long time.

Logical consequences

Rosie's mum had had enough. She said, 'We will have to walk up the escalator, and you will have to help carry the heavy bags.'

It was a very long escalator.

Rosie was outraged. 'What do you mean I will have to walk?! I don't want to walk all the way up there with these heavy bags!'

Rosie's mum replied, 'Well, it's either that or stay put and wait again. But the man can't come back for at least an hour.' She walked away and started climbing the escalator. Reluctantly, Rosie followed. She moaned all the way to the top. It was a very long, sweaty climb.

The next time they were at the shopping centre, Rosie went to press the red button again, but in the nick of time, she remembered how she had felt with the heavy bags on that sweaty climb.

She put her hand back in her pocket.

Are you intervening to 'protect the child' from the natural consequence? For example, child throws phone, breaks it, and you buy them a new phone? Yes? Then you are reinforcing their belief and understanding of the world – that whatever they do has *no* consequence and they make *no* impact on the world. No new synapses there then!

Are you going to allow an event to (safely) occur (and refrain from intervening), in order to let your child's brain grow some new synapses, and to link cause and effect? Yes?

Then you are allowing a *natural* consequence to happen.

Are you offering nurture and empathy around these naturally occurring consequences? For example, 'I can see you are sad that you lost your phone. Would you like a hug?'

Yes? Then you are practising Therapeutic Parenting with *natural* consequences and nurture. You are a brain surgeon.

Consequences need to be natural and logical and as a result of a choice the child has made. Taking things away from a child who has already lost everything is pointless and again gives them the message that they are undeserving, thus resulting in further shame and confirming the child's negative internal working model. Taking an iPad away from a child who has kicked the dog does not link cause and effect thinking in the child's brain and will never alter the behaviour!

Allowing a child to experience natural and logical consequences with nurture, helps them to link cause and effect.

6

Where Did *That* Come From?!

Sometimes, everything seems to be going very well. Our children appear settled and we feel like we are making progress.

Then, suddenly, out of the blue, a behaviour emerges, or re-emerges. A tantrum appears from nowhere. We feel like we have gone backwards.

It can be a real struggle to work out where the triggers for these behaviours are coming from and why we sometimes seem to take one step forwards, then several back!

37

The Trapdoor

(Triggers)

> I've been very confused about my child. It's almost as
> though he is two people. One minute he's present and
> engaging with us, and then suddenly his eyes darken and
> he appears to be elsewhere. He reacts to us as if we are
> other people. What on earth is going on?

Robert was playing with his mum on the living room floor. They had been playing with Lego bricks together since lunch and although Robert was tired, he was really enjoying himself.

He began to feel a bit uncomfortable and decided to move onto the rug behind him. As he touched the rug his hand got a bit caught. He felt a sliding sensation.

His mum asked him if he was ok and he was about to answer when, all of a sudden, the rug gave way and Robert fell through a hidden trapdoor. He fell so quickly that he couldn't catch the sides to break his fall.

He fell into a very dark place. Lots of loud shouty voices filled his ears and he couldn't breathe properly. His chest tightened. He could smell a strangely familiar smell of wee and rotten food and began to feel very, very frightened. As the shouty voices grew louder and drew closer, his heart pounded in his chest and he hit out in the dark, trying to protect himself. He thrashed and spun around as a voice screamed from behind him, his terror growing by the second. He grabbed hold of things he felt lying at his feet and threw them at the invisible predators. He felt a piercing scream leave his lips and then nothing...

A while later, he was astonished as he realized he was back in the living room with his mum. He found himself in a heap in the corner of the room. Toys were strewn around him and Mum had a big red mark on her cheek. 'It's ok, Robert,' he heard her say, 'you're safe now.'

Robert looked around fearfully for the other people, the shouting, the smells and all the horrible things. But they were gone. Robert sat with Mum, feeling his heart pounding. He hoped he would not fall into the scary room again, but he had a feeling he probably would.

Children who have experienced trauma struggle to differentiate between past and present.

They can be living with us in the present, then be catapulted back into the past and experience this as if it's actually happening again. It is almost like an invisible trapdoor has opened beneath them.

Their realities merge and it becomes impossible for them to be aware that they are no longer in danger. There can be known or unknown triggers when this happens.

Therapeutic Parents need to work out what the triggers are and gently bring them back into the present.

> **Traumatized children are unable to differentiate between what's *happened* and what's *happening*.**

38

Trauma Pancakes

(Multiple Issues Surfacing)

Why is it that as soon as we appear to have resolved one issue, another surfaces?

The social worker said that things should be getting easier now that Jesse has been with us for almost a year. I'm obviously doing something wrong then!

Sam had to move in with Julie and Sue. They were very nice people. Sam always had a heavy feeling in his stomach. It never went away.

The previous people Sam had lived with cared very much about him, but the social worker said they 'just couldn't cope with the pancakes!'

Julie and Sue hadn't got a clue what they were on about. As far as they could see, Sam was polite and helpful and they hadn't seen any problems regarding pancakes. 'Silly people,' they said.

One day Sam woke up feeling very happy in his new home. Then he got a dreadful tummy ache.

Julie asked Sam what he'd eaten, but as he opened his mouth, a pancake popped out. 'Wow,' said Julie, 'no wonder you've had a tummy ache. That's a big pancake.'

As she looked closer, she noticed the words 'scared of adults' etched into the pancake. Julie told Sue they would need to make sure they were consistent and safe so that Sam's fear reduced.

Everything seemed to settle again, but Julie noticed that food was disappearing from the cupboards. Then one day Sue found two pancakes hidden behind the sofa! Written on the pancakes were the words 'not being fed' on one and 'confusion' on the other. Julie and Sue did all they could to reassure Sam about food and brought in lots of new strategies to help him feel less confused too.

Julie and Sue were advised by the social worker to clear the cupboards of all flour, eggs, butter and milk, just to be on the safe side. Surely this would stop Sam being able to make pancakes?

Many months passed and Sue and Julie became more confident they'd never have to deal with another pancake episode again!

Sam was settled. He found himself feeling bursts of happiness. The bad things had stopped. He even began to feel like he might love Sue and Julie. He certainly had a nice warm feeling when they were with him.

As soon as he had this thought, he brought up a huge pancake. It said 'unworthy' on it. Sam writhed in pain as he realized he needed to show Sue and Julie he was not worthy of their love.

Julie said to Sue, 'How has this happened? There have been

no pancake ingredients in the house for weeks and now we're inundated again! I thought we had sorted everything out.'

Trauma is stacked, and much of what we see in the early days with our children is only the tip of the iceberg. Layers of trauma surface as they feel safe enough to let us 'see' them.

Therapeutic Parents recognize this and acknowledge that things often get worse before they get better. We find ourselves resolving one issue only for it to be replaced with another.

It takes years to work through the layers, and often supporting professionals fail to see this.

Parents can feel blamed, misunderstood or a failure as their child's fear-based behaviours increase.

As safety comes in, trauma comes up!

39

The Jigsaw Child

(Why Sabotage Happens)

> My child seems to be really happy about treats, etc., but then can't help himself spoiling them for everyone.

Toby was made up of lots of different parts. He didn't need to look in the mirror to know that some parts of him didn't fit very well. Sometimes the parts of the jigsaw inside him rubbed against each other and felt really uncomfortable.

When his parents said they would take them out for a lovely treat, it seemed to him that some of the jigsaw pieces got bigger and swelled up. They didn't fit any more and seem to pop out.

The treat did not fit in his jigsaw so Toby made sure that he spoiled it for everybody.

He sulked and hung back so that everyone had to wait for him. When they were out, he moaned and whined about everything.

On the way home his parents said, 'Well, we're not doing that again! You are so ungrateful!'

Toby felt his jigsaw piece shrinking back and fitting in a bit better. He felt comfortable again and understood the world.

The next day, Toby was doing some drawings at school. He put them in his book-bag to bring them home, because the teacher said he had to. (He had wanted to throw them in the bin.)

When he got home, his mum said, 'Wow that is a brilliant drawing! I'm going to put it on the fridge.'

Toby felt his jigsaw moving about inside him. The bit that said he did a 'brilliant drawing' didn't seem to fit very well. He got a big black crayon and coloured in the picture so you couldn't see it any more. Once he had done it, he looked at the black picture and he could feel the jigsaw puzzle fitting back together again inside him. 'Phew,' he thought, 'that feels better.'

When we put lots of effort into making nice times for our children, or giving them praise, we can inadvertently create a fracture in their internal working model.

We also see this in sabotaging behaviours and in obsessions. For example, a child might focus all their energy on a desired object and become fixated on it. Then, when they have the object, it is often discarded. This is because it has served its purpose. The *getting* of the object created a diversion from negative thoughts.

In the same way, a nice treat is a welcome diversion, but then those feelings of low self-worth come back in, and the child has to remind us of that.

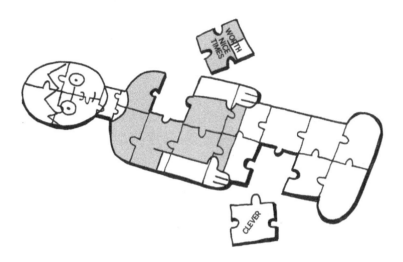

Our children can't help raining on our parade: Therapeutic Parents need big umbrellas.

40

The Smoke Detector

(Unexpected Behaviours)

My child always seems to be right on the edge. She can be simmering and ready to pop at any moment!

When Sophie was a baby, she had a smoke detector. The smoke detector was very useful when there was actual danger, like a real fire. But unfortunately, this smoke detector was faulty.

It became faulty from over-use.

First of all, it just went off when there was actual smoke. The smoke was special smoke. It came from people arguing, loud voices, bangs and other frightening things.

Sophie got a bit tired of all the noise from the smoke detector. She never felt like she could relax. She became watchful. She worked hard to keep smoke away from the smoke detector. She smiled a lot at the shouty people so the smoke detector wouldn't go off. It always made her jump and she was always on the look-out for smoke.

The smoke detector started going off all the time. Even when there was just a bit of steam from people talking loudly, it would overreact and send out its shrill alarm.

It made Sophie's head shake.

When Sophie moved to a new house, she hoped that the smoke detector would calm down a bit, but the smoke detector was so used to sensing danger everywhere that it would be set off at the slightest thing. Sophie put her hands over her ears. She couldn't stand it!

Luckily, in her new house there lived a Therapeutic Parent. The Therapeutic Parent knew how to reset faulty smoke detectors. Each time the alarm went off, she would come and reset it.

Over the next few years the Therapeutic Parent gradually re-wired the faulty smoke detector.

Sophie was so happy when she finally realized that the smoke detector was no longer faulty. Nowadays it only went off when there was a real emergency.

Children from trauma have overdeveloped cortisol and adrenalin responses, making them ready to over-react to even mild stimuli. They are often watchful, especially where frightening things have happened to them multiple times.

Their brains start to work like faulty smoke detectors, sensing danger everywhere. This is exhausting for the child *and* the parent.

Instead of resetting, do re-wiring.

41

The Monster in the Cupboard

(Difficult Quiet Times)

Sometimes bedtime is going well and my child seems settled. Then he is up and down, talking about the most ridiculous things and general avoiding bedtime. What do I do?

Teddy does not like thinking about the memory monster in the cupboard. The monster is made up of all the bad things that happened. Teddy has a cupboard in his mind and he locks the monster away in it.

The monster is not happy to be in the cupboard and makes lots of banging noises. Teddy can normally manage this as he keeps really busy and makes loads of noise. That way he can't hear the monster. But he knows he's still there.

Teddy knows that the memory monster is very big and strong. Teddy works really hard to keep the monster locked away. He knows that the more attention he pays to the monster, the stronger it gets.

The worst time is at night or at quiet times. When there is nothing to do, Teddy can hear the memory monster tapping inside his head. Sometimes the tapping is really loud.

Sometimes Teddy gives the monster something to keep it busy. This is monster bait. When the monster is busy with the monster bait, it is not bothering Teddy. Some things Teddy uses as monster bait are arguments, fighting, eating lots of food, stealing things and keeping very busy with his friends, doing dangerous things.

The monster bait gets him in trouble. Teddy doesn't care. At least it stops the memory monster getting out of the cupboard and bothering him.

Since Teddy has been living with Geoff and Emma, they have been helping him to deal with the monster. At bedtime, they know they need to stay with him and play quiet music, or just stay close and hold his hand.

One day, Teddy knows that with Geoff and Emma's help, the monster won't bother him anymore.

A lot of our children struggle with bad memories. We see this in their behaviour where they find it difficult to settle at night, or to be still and quiet.

Our children often tend to create a little chaos or focus on distractions to keep their thoughts away from the invading memories. We need to recognize that it is the trauma which is stopping our children from settling, and help them to regulate by staying close and letting them know that we understand what is going on.

To help your child with this issue, see our children's story, *Teddy Tappy and the Tangley Memory Monster*.[1]

> **Your child's behaviour is a communication about their inner distress.**

---

1 Sarah Naish (2018) *Teddy Tappy and the Tangley Memory Monster*. Createspace Independent Publishing Platform Ltd.

7

The Overwhelming Need

Therapeutic Parents rarely wake up in the morning and think, 'It's such a lovely day! I wonder what we should do today?'

Our lives are constrained by needing to think about everything, from all angles, all the time. We have to think about what might happen if we take a course of action. How the children might respond, what happened last time? I call this 'double thinking' and it's exhausting!

The level of need our children have can seem overwhelming. The behaviours are relentless and we are often left feeling that it is up to *us* to sort it all out, all the time. It is not an easy life!

42

The Two-Year-Old Psychopath

(Lack of Empathy)

My child has no thought, care or empathy for anyone but himself. He steals, lies and just does whatever he wants to do all the time.

I am very worried. I think my grandson, Jack, is a psychopath. He is two. I know it is early to worry about this. Why would I say this?

Well, for a start he has no empathy whatsoever.

Recently, we sadly lost our little black dog, Mabel. She was 14 years old and had always been with our family. When Jack noticed that Mabel was missing, I gently told him that she had died and gone to heaven. Jack then asked for a 'new black dog'! No care for how I might be feeling and clearly no attachment to poor Mabel!

Then there is the stealing.

I went to the supermarket with him and he just blatantly took a banana and started trying to eat it. I took him to the store manager and apologized. I couldn't believe it when the manager just laughed and ruffled Jack's head. What kind of lesson is that?!

And as for lying...well!

The other day Jack told me he was a firefighter. This is such a blatant lie. Just because he was dressed up in a dressing-up outfit and riding a toy engine did *not* make him an actual firefighter. I told him this, but he would not have it.

And the violence!

Last week Jack got out a toy sword and started bashing all his teddies. I was horrified. I phoned the police to try to teach him a lesson, but they would not even come and talk to him.

And he takes such risks...

Yesterday we were walking near the road and he tried to run in the road in front of an actual car. He did not seem to care in the slightest that he could have been hurt. He laughed!

Is the two-year-old grandson a psychopath? No, of course not. He is showing age and developmental stage appropriate behaviour.

When our children from trauma become stuck at age two developmentally, we see the same behaviours. They need to go through the stage they missed.

This does not make them evil, psychopaths, sociopaths or anything else. It makes them children who are stuck and need our help.

An unmet need remains unmet until it's met.

43

The Pet Spider

(Being Controlled)

> I can't do Therapeutic Parenting! I feel like they are getting away with it all the time and I am just running round in circles. I am exhausted!

You may recall that in Chapters 2 and 3 we explained how children from trauma are scared of adults (Spider Parents), and how sometimes they can be overly friendly. Well, there is another side to this too, which can be exhausting for parents!

When Felix moved in with his new Spider Parents, they smiled at him a lot and said he could trust them.

Felix was not stupid. He had trusted the last Spider Parents and look what happened there! Felix knew that really he needed to be in control of them.

He started making a lovely cage for the spiders to go into. He quite fancied the idea of having a pet spider.

He began controlling the Spider Parents by telling everyone what to do. They soon fell in line when he did a bit of fake crying too! He changed where everyone sat at the table, what they ate and when. He would decide that he liked some food one day, but the next day said it made him sick. He enjoyed watching the Spider Parents run around trying to find something he would eat. It made him smile in his head.

The Spider Parents thought they were helping Felix to feel 'empowered'. They did not know that he was feeling less and less safe and more and more threatened by them.

He wanted to go out whenever he pleased, but the annoying Spider Parents followed him. Felix knew what to do. He tied the Spider Parents' legs in a big wriggly knot. He did this by making sure he stayed out long enough for everyone to be really scared and agree to anything he wanted when he returned. It was hilarious!

Another way Felix controlled his Spider Parents was by being really scary; he knew he could squash them any time he wanted to, and his spider parents always seemed to want to make Felix calm. He used this to his maximum advantage. Every time he hit them or tried to squash them, they just kept saying stupid things like 'I can see you're very angry at the moment,' as they ran away!

Eventually, Felix felt that he had built a very nice cage, which he allowed the Spider Parents to live in. They were now his pet spiders. He gave his pet spiders a little exercise wheel in the cage so they could have fun running round and round in circles. He thought that was really great!

He was able to see where they were at all times, and Felix was in charge. Brilliant!

The Spider Parents did not know what had happened. They were exhausted, scared, bruised and battered. They felt trapped. 'Where did we go wrong?' they asked each other.

If we are unable to keep to a strong routine and maintain clear boundaries, life quickly descends into chaos!

Sometimes it feels easier to give up and just let the child get their way 'for a quiet life'. When we do this, we are creating flexible boundaries which make our children feel unsafe.

Therapeutic Parenting is underpinned with firm boundaries and structure and we *must* ensure that we keep our children within those boundaries and remain the unassailable safe base with a steady consistency.

Our children can only have control if we choose to give it to them.

44

Memory Beach

(Memory Issues)

I have to remember every little thing for my child. He often does not remember things from one day to the next. I feel like his PA!

The little boy was really happy at school. He was enjoying learning all about the Vikings. At the end of the school day, he put everything he had learnt about the Vikings into a special box.

Later that day he went for a walk with his mum on the beach. The beach was really exciting. The little boy put the box with all the special things about the Vikings in it on the sand and went to play in the sea.

The next day at school the teacher said, 'Right, we are going to see what you remember about the Vikings.'

The little boy vaguely remembered the name, and searched frantically for the box holding all the information. Everything he had learned about the Vikings was in that box. He felt panicky and sweaty. He looked around and the other children were all really happy, clearly having all the information they needed.

The little boy said to the teacher, 'I don't remember anything about the Vikings, I've lost my memory box!'

The teacher looked really surprised and replied, 'But you had everything yesterday. I gave it to you. You had all the information!'

That evening the little boy went down to the beach. The tide was in and there was no sign of the little memory box with all the things in about the Vikings. The little boy was sad. He felt that all that information was gone forever. He wondered how many other boxes he had lost. He couldn't remember.

In the distance he saw another box on the shoreline. He ran up to it and opened it. Inside there were lots of pictures and stories about a lovely day out he had had with his family when they went to the zoo. The little boy sat and looked at all the things. He was really pleased he had those great memories back again.

He took the little case and went home to his mum. He told her that he had all the memories back about the picnic. His mum said, 'That's funny. When we spoke about that last week, you didn't remember it and now it's come back again!'

'Yes,' said the little boy, 'I've realized what happens: My memories go in and out with the sea and I never know what it's going to wash up or when.'

Looking after children who struggle to remember is hard for parents! Not only do our children forget everyday things, meaning they become disorganized, but sometimes big, important events are forgotten.

It can be very disappointing for a parent to work hard giving a child a lovely time, only to find the memory is washed away without trace.

Don't despair though. You never know when those memories will wash back up. They are still out there bobbing about!

Being your child's memory organizer makes life easier for you and them!

45

The Hand-Grenade

(The 'Trouble-Maker')

I get so tired because I have to be with the children all the time. There always seems to be a fight or an argument when I am not with them. I am constantly refereeing.

The children were all sitting quietly watching TV with Dad. All was harmonious. Even the dogs were asleep.

As it approached 5:30, Dad said, 'Right, I am just going to put the dinner on.'

Katie didn't like it when Dad left the room. It made her feel a bit wobbly. She looked at her brother and sister, staring intently at the screen. She felt invisible.

'I know what to do,' she thought, 'I'll use one of my emergency attention hand-grenades.'

Katie got the hand-grenade out of her pocket and pulled the pin. 'I know what we are having for dinner,' she said. Her brother and sister looked at her suspiciously.

'It had better not be spaghetti bolognese,' said Sam. 'I hate spaghetti bolognese!'

Katie threw the hand-grenade at Sam. 'Well, it *is* spaghetti bolognese and it's my favourite! Yay!'

The hand-grenade made Sam erupt. He flew across the room, shouting at Katie. She screamed, 'Dad, Dad! He's punching me!'

Dad came back in and saw Sam shouting. Sam was very angry. 'You are a fat idiot! I hate you all!' he screamed.

Dad was very cross. He had been trying to make the dinner. He told Sam to calm down. Katie smiled and said, 'I am calm, Daddy. Shall I help you make the dinner?'

Dad was instantly suspicious. He looked around, and sure enough, there was the empty hand-grenade near where Sam had been sitting.

'Hmm,' he said, 'I think I see what happened here. Katie was worried I had forgotten about her when I went to make dinner, so she said something for Sam to make a big fuss. Come here both of you and let's have a cuddle.'

Katie went bright red. She was sure she had hidden the hand-grenade really well. It seemed to her that Dad knew everything.

It can truly be overwhelming, the level of need our children have for our attention. It sometimes feels like we cannot get five minutes' peace!

When there is arguing and fighting, it's important to try not to referee. Once you fall into this trap, your children will keep you firmly in that place.

When children throw 'attention hand-grenades', it can make our lives a lot easier if we identify the source and tackle it head on. If we keep responding to the *recipient* of the grenade, the grenades will keep being thrown!

Remember to look for who *threw* the hand grenade, not the recipient!

46

The Car Crash

(Feeling Overwhelmed)

> Sometimes I feel completely overwhelmed by my children's needs. They seem so huge and I am so ill-equipped!

I went out for a walk as it was a sunny day. My walk took me down a very quiet lane, off the beaten track. As I rounded the corner I was horrified to see that two cars had collided! I didn't know how long they had been there, but there were people inside. I ran towards them and quickly realized that this was worse than I thought. There were three passengers in one car and one in the other. Two of the passengers were bleeding profusely; one clearly had a terrible head injury and was shouting in pain. One was unconscious. It did not look good. I tried to ring 999, but there was no signal.

I had done a first-aid course, but nothing had prepared me for this! In my bag I had a box of plasters. I got the plasters out and looked at them. I looked at all the injured people.

I had a terrible thought! There was nothing I could do. Should I just walk past and pretend I had not seen this car crash? I looked again at my box of plasters and thought about my course. Nothing came into my head. I was overwhelmed with panic and thoughts of escaping this horror. I was not equipped to deal with this. Surely no one could blame me? The plasters could not make any difference. I could not possibly deal with this alone.

As I went to sneak away, convincing myself that it was better not to get involved, and save myself the trauma, I looked back and saw one of the injured passengers looking terrified.

I knew then that there *was* something I could do after all. I could tell them someone had seen them, run to get a signal, then return to stay with them, reassure them, give them hope and do what I could.

The plasters would never be enough. But I could still make a difference.

It is easy to feel overwhelmed by our children's needs. It often seems like whatever training or previous experience we had, it is now irrelevant. We find ourselves alone, facing what looks like a catastrophe.

Sometimes we might even believe that we are making things worse with our attempts to help.

We may well be ill-equipped and feel like we are in over our heads. It can be a very lonely and frightening place to be.

In the next section we have some analogies to help cope with these feelings.

> **We may not be equipped with the right tools, but we can always make a difference.**

8

Filling the Cup

It's so important that Therapeutic Parents – well, *all* parents – take time to look after themselves. It can be really easy to put our own needs second.

I often hear from parents who are exhausted and over-whelmed, yet when they are offered the chance to meet up with a local Listening Circle or supporter, they cancel at the last minute, or they don't turn up.

It can feel as if there is always a reason not to go, or a last-minute emergency, or maybe even the children just behaving in such a way to try and stop the parent leaving the house!

Yet it is worth trying to prioritize. Even a few minutes speaking to someone who gets it, and sharing the burden, makes such a huge difference to parents. We need to take care of ourselves first!

47

The Empty Cup

(Exhaustion)

> Life is too hard. If I get five minutes, I just want to sit in a dark room. It's too much hassle to do all this self-care nonsense. The children take up all my time.

The child arrived holding a polystyrene cup. There was a tiny bit of water left in the bottom in case the child got thirsty. As Samantha got closer, she saw that the cup was full of holes. The holes had things written around them like, 'always hungry', 'scared of adults', and 'no routine'.

Samantha said, 'Wow you must be thirsty! Let me fill your cup up for you.' She took out her own polystyrene cup, which was brimming with positive energy. She tipped it into the child's cup.

The water poured out of all the holes in the child's cup. The child looked at Samantha with an 'I told you so' look on his face.

Every day Samantha tried to fill the cup for the child, and every day the water she put in just poured out of the holes. She noticed that her own cup started to get holes in it. Her positive energy was leaking out. The holes had writing around like, 'exhausted, frustrated, out of ideas'.

Samantha's friend, Jess, phoned her up and said, 'Come out with us, we're all meeting for a coffee.'

'I can't,' said Samantha, 'I am just too exhausted. My cup has run out and there are holes all over it. I can't fill it up anymore.'

Samantha sat in her house looking sadly at her cup full of holes. She looked at the child next to her, still holding tightly to his nearly empty cup, also full of holes. Samantha realized their cups looked almost the same.

Suddenly there was a knock at the door. It was Jess. She was holding a big jug of positive energy water and a box of plasters.

'Right!' she said. 'Give me your cup a moment.'

Jess took Samantha's cup and put plasters all over the holes. Samantha did not know what was going on. Jess finished putting plasters all over the holes and then filled the cup up.

Samantha looked on in astonishment. She was suddenly feeling so much better. She took a few sips of water as her friend gave her a cup of tea and a lovely slice of cake she brought round.

Samantha looked at the child sitting next to her. She realized she had some energy water in her cup and some plasters left over.

It is a sad fact that our children come to us with low resilience and a high level of need. We can run out of energy ourselves

by constantly trying to meet the overwhelming needs. We find our own resilience runs low, and we no longer seem to have the resources to meet our child's needs.

We must allow others to help us to replenish our cup, but it can be hard to find time and space to be able to do this. If we do not make sure our own needs are met, we simply cannot meet the needs of others.

Self-care is not selfish. It is essential.

You cannot pour from an empty cup.

48

The Boring Place

(Getting a Break)

> I can never go and meet friends or get out, because every time I do, I have to pay. Behaviours are dreadful before and after. It's just not worth it!

Alfie was a bit worried. It looked like Mum was going out. Alfie did not like it when Mum went out. She was putting on sparkly eyes so that was a bit of a giveaway! Alfie needed to stop Mum.

He went into his bedroom and looked around for something he could do. He spotted the fish tank. Mum liked the fish. If he helped the fish tank to fall over, Mum would probably be very busy clearing it up. That would help her to stay with him.

Mum heard the loud crash and came running to his room. She looked in horror at the fish on the floor.

It took a long time to clear up and sort out. Mum did not go out.

The next day, Mum said, 'It's a real shame but I have to go to "The Boring Place" tonight.'

Alfie was curious. 'What is "The Boring Place?"' he asked.

'Well, it's a really dull place where there are no pictures on the walls. You just have to sit and do boring sums or write the same thing over and over again.'

'Is there cake?' asked Alfie.

'No,' said Mum. 'There are only fish paste sandwiches.'

Alfie did not like fish paste sandwiches. They were disgusting.

'Is there music there?' he asked.

'No,' Mum sighed. 'There's just one long buzzing sound which never changes.'

Alfie did not like the sound of that.

'Are there other children to play with?' he asked.

'No, sadly not,' said Mum. 'There aren't even other adults to talk to. Just me, the sums and the room. The chair doesn't even spin round.'

'I know!' she said, 'Why don't you come with me? You can help me do the sums!'

'Well,' said Alfie, thinking fast, 'if I don't come, who will be here with me?'

'Daddy will be here. He was going to do pizza night but I am sure he will save you some.' Mum looked excited at the thought of Alfie coming to help her.

Alfie decided he would not go to 'The Boring Place' after all.

Mum said she really did not want to go as it would be so dull.

She had a disappointed face, but Alfie was too focused on pizza night.

Mum trudged sadly out of the door, but when she was out of sight she started skipping.

She got her sparkly eyes ready in the car.

When we need to organize time for ourselves, we really need to make sure this is not looking like a lovely time to the children!

With a little bit of foresight and planning, we can still get time away. Most children do not want to go to 'The Boring Place', especially if what is happening for them looks more interesting.

Even a short break of a couple of hours can reset the stress levels and give you clear thinking time.

Children are unlikely to want to join you in your 'Boring Place'.

49

Eeyore Parenting

(Losing Hope)

There's nothing I can do. I have lost count of the number of diagnoses my child has. He is a hopeless case.

In the film *Christopher Robin*, there is a scene in which Christopher Robin is standing on a bridge looking at the water. Eeyore appears in the river, on his back, drifting towards the waterfall. Christopher Robin sees a rocky mound sticking up and shouts at Eeyore to go to it.

'There's no point,' moans Eeyore. 'I am going over the waterfall anyway.'

Christopher Robin gets a stick to help him. Eeyore makes no effort to grab it. He continues lamenting his fate.

Isobel was also drifting down Hopeless River. Her friend Glynis offered her a way to save herself. The rocky mound was an afternoon of child care; the stick Glynis held out was information to help resolve the latest issue with Isobel's child.

'There's no point,' said Isobel as she drifted towards the waterfall. 'It's all hopeless.'

Glynis dragged Isobel out of the water. They sat on the bank looking at Hopeless River. Glynis listened to Isobel for a long time. She didn't seem to be able to hear any help from Glynis. Eventually, after lots of listening with empathy, Glynis had to take action. 'Look, Isobel,' she said, 'no one can see when you are crying into a blindfold. We all have tricky children and I know it can be very tough.'

'Not as tough as mine,' lamented Isobel. 'My child has more diagnoses than anyone else and has more difficult behaviours too!'

'Well,' said Glynis firmly, 'we can either waste time indulging in a bit of "Top Trump Hope-less Parenting" or you can use my boat!'

Isobel was curious, 'Boat?'

Glynis said, 'I have a boat. Lots of Therapeutic Parents use boats! I can lend you mine.'

She explained, 'Therapeutic Parents roll up their sleeves, drive the boat, notice that the children are drilling holes in the bottom of the boat, repair the holes swiftly (with nurture and empathy), and keep driving (maintaining structure and routine). Waterfalls are difficult but possible to navigate.'

'Unfortunately, though, "Eeyore Parents" notice the children drilling the holes, ask them to stop, negotiate, plead, get angry and, eventually, join in with drilling the holes whilst pointing out to everyone that the boat is sinking faster. Which parent would you like to be?'

Isobel said she did not know how to drive a boat.

'That's ok,' said Glynis, 'I will come with you and show you.'

We all hit bad times when everything seems futile, but sometimes our lives feel taken over and we become a hope- *less* parent!

It might be that you are in deep compassion fatigue; it might be that you are in need of empathy for yourself; it might be that you genuinely do not know what to do next.

In order to help our children, we have to stop drilling holes and instead take the patches and tools offered by others such as knowledgeable friends and the National Association of Therapeutic Parents.[1]

This may sound harsh. I have every sympathy with fatigued parents, but if we don't help ourselves we cannot help our children.

Raising our children is very tough. Our attitude to the challenge is key. Of course, we have tough times. Sometimes they seem to go on forever, but we must be the leaders, the inspiration and the force for change.

Our children cannot heal if we join them in lamenting their wounds.

---

1   www.naotp.com

50

The Rabbit

(Isolation)

> I feel so isolated, like no one can understand the life we have to lead.

Rabbit was finding life very difficult. Where he lived was dark. The sun hardly ever shone. The hardest thing, though, was dealing with his son. He never knew what he was going to do next. Sometimes he was even frightened of his own boy! Rabbit was lonely too.

Every day, Rabbit hoped a magic thing would happen, but every day he continued living his difficult life in the near dark, scared of his son, but worrying about him too.

One day a beautiful white butterfly landed right near to where Rabbit was huffing and sighing.

'Why are you huffing and sighing here in the dark?' asked the butterfly.

'Well,' replied Rabbit, 'look at it! I am so lonely, I never know what my son will do next. I have a tough, dark life.'

The butterfly was astonished! 'But you are on the dark side of the wall in the shade!' she said, 'There are loads of rabbits in the sun, just the other side!'

Rabbit was thrilled. He had had no idea that he had been leaning on a wall. He thought he'd been leaning against the 'end of the world'. He didn't know there was a brighter side!

The butterfly told him he would have to make a slight effort and dig under the wall. She showed him a little hole he could peep through first to see.

Rabbit looked through the hole. He could not believe his eyes. There was sun; there were other rabbits. He set about digging under the wall.

When he got to the other side, he felt such relief. The dig was worth the effort. He told the other rabbits how worried he was about his son, how scared he had been. He asked if they had children too. 'Oh yes,' a large rabbit replied, 'but between us we have worked out loads of ways to make things better. Come and have a chat.'

Here's what they said:

'We know that sometimes you lie awake at night worrying for your child's future.

'We know that if your child is missing, you automatically think about the worst-case scenarios, even when logically you know they are ok.

'We know that when your child is blatantly lying to your face yet again, you sometimes feel consumed with rage.

'We know that you are often exasperated, furious and desperate when the school or the social worker fails to understand the most basic issues you are dealing with on a day to day basis.

'We know that sometimes you feel that no one around you understands what you are dealing with; and worse, offers patronizing advice.

'We know that you often feel completely dumbfounded by the seemingly illogical, repetitive behaviours you are presented with.

'We know that sometimes you wake up in the morning and cannot think how you will get through the day.

'We know that some of you suffer horrendous levels of violence, yet no one seems to care.

'We know that you sometimes feel lonely, isolated, blamed, sad and out of your depth.

'And yet you continue.

'You are heroes, each and every one of you, doing the hardest job, in a system that often does not understand or support you.

'Help *is* at hand.

'You are not alone.'[1]

1   Contact the National Association of Therapeutic Parents (www.naotp.com) for support groups, advice lines, school support and Listening Circles.

Sometimes we need to make a tiny effort to circumvent the 'end of the world' and find 'the bright side'.

51

The Empathy Bowl

(Effective Listening)

I'm sick and tired of not being listened to! When my other half comes home from work, if I tell him what's been happening, he thinks I'm just being moody or need him to give me the answers! I feel like he's shutting me down!

Mrs Frog was very fed up.

She had many problems and everyone else in the pond was getting on her nerves, particularly all the tadpoles! She would hop from lily pad to lily pad looking for someone to listen to her but to no avail.

Mrs Croak was a miserable old so-and-so, always complaining about everything and never letting anyone else get a word in edgeways.

Mr Reptile's young ones were, apparently, perfect!

Ms Toad was full of advice, but Mrs Frog always left feeling like a failure.

Mrs Frog was just about to jump ponds when Mrs Leap came to her aid. Mrs Leap had recently attended training on helping amphibians in distress. She sat alongside Mrs Frog and held out an enormous bowl tightly weaved from beautiful pond grass.

Mrs Frog asked what the bowl was for. 'This is an empathy bowl, my dear,' said Mrs Leap.

'I will sit and hold the bowl for you to pour all your troubles into. All your worries, your burdens and your woes. This bowl can take them all and I am strong enough to carry them.'

Mrs Frog sat with Mrs Leap and her bowl for a very long time. She emptied out all her troubles into the bowl. As the bowl began to fill, she felt lighter. Mrs Leap nodded occasionally, reassuring Mrs Frog that it was ok to be totally fed up, and encouraging her to keep filling the bowl.

Afterwards Mrs Frog felt so much better. She felt she had been listened to; but most of all, she felt she could face another day.

Once the bowl had been filled, she was also even able to remember and use some of the helpful advice Ms Toad had offered.

Looking after children who have experienced trauma is a full-time job. It can be relentlessly tiring and parents are at significant risk of experiencing compassion fatigue and burnout. Going to work is like having 'respite'. Connecting with other adults in reciprocal relationships or working alone in peace and quiet can provide a much-needed break.

If you or your partner have a job outside of the home, it is important to leave work at the door. Maybe stop for a coffee on the way home to shake off the dust of the day.

Upon arrival at home, try not to judge or move into offering 'helpful advice'. Imagine an invisible Empathy Bowl at the door. Pick it up and hold it whilst listening and empathizing. Allow your partner to offload the woes of the day into the bowl. Offer to make them a drink, bathe the children, etc. This will enable your partner to reconnect with you, and you might even get the opportunity to offer that 'helpful advice' after all.

Hold the invisible Empathy Bowl for those who need us to listen.

9

Hope

It can be very easy for us to slide into a thinking pattern where we imagine a future without hope.

And yet, we continue.

Why is that? Could it be that there are those around us who have gone before, shone a light and said, 'Come on, keep going you will be fine?'

Hope and humour are what keep us all going. They are our best friends in the darkest of times.

52

The Twisty-Turny Steps

(Fear for the Future)

I am so scared for my child's future. If he carries on the way he is, he will end up with no qualifications, on drugs, in prison or even worse.

I did not realize how twisted this path would be. There are so many steps on it and so many winding turns. Sometimes I can't imagine that we will ever get to the top. I've trudged up the steps one at a time. Often a step is missing and I need to put more effort in to keep climbing.

I can't see the top and I can't imagine what the top looks like. We've been going up these twisty-turny steps for so long now that that's all I really remember.

I think it's all my child remembers too. The steps are much steeper for him than they are for me because his legs are much smaller. At least I'm confident that one day we will get somewhere and that up is the right direction.

On the bad days I stop and look behind me and then I can see how far we have come. It really is quite amazing when you see the distance we have travelled. Sometimes I forget to do that.

Often I worry that my child is going to just stop halfway or even start going back down again; but as long as I keep a firm hold of his hand and keep going upwards, he will follow me.

Sometimes I'm scared that if he misses steps out he will go down a different path – one that goes towards drugs, prison, alcohol or dangerous others. That's when I am looking too far ahead. That's when I see the steps are disappearing off into the distance. And I am imagining the worst.

Catastrophic thinking is when we constantly look too far ahead and panic about our children's futures.

Often, we find it so hard to visualize where we are going on this tough, steep, twisting path.

But if we concentrate on taking one step at a time (and dealing only with what is in front of us), we can sometimes take a pause and look back at how far we have come.

Then, one day, we are standing at the top with our children and looking all the way down and suddenly realizing what we have all overcome.

When the future is too frightening, deal with what is in front of you today.

53

The Diet Fail

(Having a Bad Day)

I've completely blown it. I lost my temper and feel dreadful. My poor child. I've ruined everything again!

You know those times when you've been really, really good on your diet for days!?

You've denied yourself, you've stuck to the rules; you are feeling very positive about your progress. You've lost loads of weight already and you are feeling fitter.

And then you blow it. You have a whole packet of biscuits, a bar of chocolate and basically anything else you can stuff your face with.

It feels so good, you cannot stop.

And then the guilt, the low, the disappointment in yourself, the feeling of 'Well, I've blown it now so I might as well carry on.' You feel as if all the good work you have done has been undone. Your stomach feels bloated.

You accept that you were probably born to be fat.

But wait!

Are you physically bigger today? No, you are not.

Do you get on the scales and see that you have put on a stone today? No, you do not.

Have you actually gone up three sizes in clothes?

No.

It was just a bad day.

When you have a bad day with your children, after trying so hard and doing so well for so long, it's tempting to fall into the same trap!

'I can't do it. I've blown it now! There's no point.'

Well, guess what?

The connections you built yesterday still exist! All the safe days and bonds you have made are still there. You haven't damaged your children for life because you were snappy, grumpy or shouted.

You may even have taught your child that you can be angry, repair and still keep them safe.

Today will definitely end and you can comfort yourself with the fact that you tried. And if you didn't try, you tried on a different day....and you can try again in the future.

Every time we do a therapeutic response with our children, linking cause and effect, we build loads of new synapses. You might not have built loads today but you have in the past and they are still there. They don't die off because you are having a bad day.

This is very fortunate as otherwise my children's brain lights would have gone out by now.

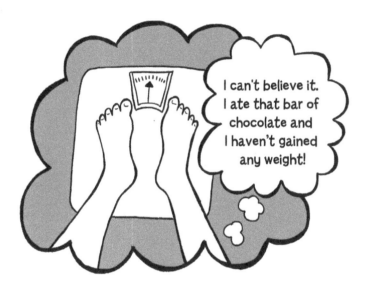

The synapses you lit last week did not go out in your child's brain because you had a bad day.

54

Slides and Ladders

(Overcoming Obstacles)

I often feel like we take one step forwards then ten big steps back! This happens especially when we have contact and it goes badly.

Life with our children can feel a bit like snakes and ladders, but more like 'Slides and Ladders!'

You and your child begin on the first square and throw your dice in turns. Things appear to be going in your favour as you throw your die and move six squares. Your child takes their turn and lags a few squares behind. After another throw she catches up with you and you're now on the same square. You feel satisfied that you're neck and neck but are more than happy to allow your child to win the game as long as you're right behind them. Unfortunately, she then throws the die again and lands on the top of a slide. In the square it says 'contact'.

After a difficult contact with her birth family, she has fallen all the way back down to square one. You know there is a ladder a few squares along and desperately hope that she gets there quickly. You throw your die and also land on the top of the slide. You slide down all the way to the bottom to be with your child. Both of you are very disappointed, but you try to reassure your child you'll soon both get to a ladder and find your way back to the top. The main thing is that you are together.

You get to the ladder before your child and find yourself at the top again willing your child to join you soon. It is usually the case that you recover more quickly.

Sadly, your child passes the ladder and falls down yet another slide. You are waiting for the fallout. You know she doesn't like losing and offer to swap places. Your child refuses, stating she doesn't need your help to get back up to the top and she'll find her own ladder in her own time. You are worried she might not do this; it all seems as if the chips are stacked against her, and you're willing her to quickly throw a four and climb back up a ladder. She will still be quite a way behind, but you'll do your best to angle your die in order to stay close by when she eventually lands on the correct square. It's all down to chance, but surely she'll eventually catch up, even if it takes a long time?

Your child is now just a square behind you and there is only one slide left in front. You're convinced she'll jump over it and win the game. Unfortunately she doesn't and falls back down a slide again. This time, however, she only falls to the row beneath as the slides are shorter the further you move along the board. You notice that your child isn't complaining as much this time as she is now beginning to learn that there is a way back to the top and she'll eventually get there as long as you are patient and reassure her that there is always a ladder after every slide.

Parents are often convinced that their children are doing very well, then something happens and it appears as if all your hard work has been pointless and you're back where you started.

This couldn't be further from the truth. Your child can easily regress back into their younger self. They may have been triggered by a sudden or unexpected change, contact, an alteration in routine, meeting a new person, or maybe they are just having a bad day. They haven't gone all the way back to the beginning; they have had a difficult time and are struggling to stay on track. This is due to the fragmentation of the child and inability to self-regulate. The Therapeutic Parent needs to be the child's unassailable safe base, coming alongside and helping the child to get back up to where they need to be. You will already have a whole arsenal of tools which you use without thinking. These tools can quickly help your child to re-establish their equilibrium.

Consistency of parental responses, predictability of routine and the reliability of empathy and nurture enable the child to get back on track.

When your child falls down a slide, remember you have the ladder!

55

The Trauma Lake

(Foundations for Change)

> Sometimes it feels like nothing I do ever makes any difference. When will I see a change?

247

Imagine you are standing on a shoreline with a still, flat lake in front of you. It's called Trauma Lake. Every time you try an intervention, or resolve a difficult day, you are throwing a rock in that lake.

It makes a few ripples, but after a few moments, nothing has changed, and it feels as though you have not made any difference to the landscape. You are back where you started.

But what is happening to those rocks you are throwing in? Well, they land somewhere on the bed of the Trauma Lake. The rocks are made from:

empathic responses
taking that breath before you launch in
the structure and routine you relied on
the little nurture bombs you put in
the wondering aloud
naming the unspoken needs
meeting the unmet needs.

Every time you throw a rock in, every Therapeutic Parenting intervention you do is a solid rock, a building block being put in place.

Our children's Trauma Lake might be deep. We may need to give them life jackets to help them while we are getting the rocks in. The life jackets are made from acceptance and an alternative version of their future.

Sometimes you might find that you are also in the Trauma Lake. You need a life jacket too. Your life jacket is made from hope, empathic friends, humour and determination.

Over the years, the lake may look dark and forbidding, but then you realize that the sun is shining behind you. The rocks start to break the surface of the water, and you see a different child in a different landscape.

All that time...and you thought nothing was changing.

Your children cannot surface above Trauma Lake without the building blocks you put in there first.

56

The Hidden Path

(Inspiration)

> I feel like I have lost my way. I am not even sure I am doing the right things for my child. I don't know where we are going.

Rosie and her mum, Sarah, started their walk in the sunshine. The path ahead looked clear and bright. Sometimes the path got a little steep, sometimes it went downhill, but it was always laid out before them.

Sarah kept a firm grasp of Rosie's hand to make sure she stayed on the path. Rosie was not too thrilled about that. She quite fancied going off the path and often tried to pull Sarah off.

It didn't work.

One day a deep fog fell. It was so thick they could hardly see where they were going. Rosie was quite scared. Whenever she was scared, she became rude and angry.

Sarah looked down at her feet and could not see the path at all. She looked ahead and could not see where they were going anymore. She noticed Rosie's rude and angry face, but more importantly, she saw the scared little girl.

'It's fine,' she said. 'Come on, we will just keep feeling the way with our feet.'

After quite a lot of walking and tight hand-holding, the fog began to clear. They both saw a vague outline of the path. Sarah was very relieved they had managed to stay on the path.

Rosie was very glad she had continued holding Mum's hand.

You know those days when you think you are getting somewhere, then something happens? Your child goes backwards. Their trauma resurfaces in a behaviour you thought you had left behind ages ago. Or a new difficult behaviour surfaces.

You feel like you are getting nowhere, despite all this work, years and years of effort, therapy, patience, trying to be insightful and working things through.

You feel like a failure as a parent. A fraud. People tell you that you are doing so well, but you don't feel it. You see the evidence of your child's trauma every day. It is overwhelming.

Take heart. You are walking a path with your child, and every day you are taking a step on that path.

Have faith. You are heading in the right direction. Keep your eyes focused on where you are heading and keep going. Keep holding your child's hand. One step in front of the other.

Just because you cannot always see the path, it doesn't mean it is not there.